Dedication

This book is dedicated to a true "Raider of the Lost Ark," James Whittall of Rowley, Massachusetts. He has been called, among other things, a "maverick archaeologist," and if that means that he has the courage to challenge the complacent and investigate radical theories of other historians and archaeologists, then he is indeed a maverick. His research and field probings have forced the masters of the field to open their eyes wider, dig beyond their noses, and change some of their hard-nosed opinions. One of his many accomplishments was to found America's Early Sites Research Society, a non-profit organization that shares its vast wealth of research and experience with you and me — giving us a deeper insight into the intriguing mysteries of the ancient world. He is our Indiana Jones.

Jim Whittall at his home office in Rowley, Massachusetts. Off the beaten path, his home is a combination museum, library, and research lab, where only he can find anything.

COVER PHOTO: Shown is a monolith at summer solstice sunset, Mystery Hill, America's Stonehenge, North Salem, New Hampshire. Photo by Brian Sullivan.

Glossary of Terms

Archaeologists live in a world apart from ours and have a language of their own. Therefore, I thought it best to provide meanings of some words which are used in this book and in the general chit-chat of archaeologists.

Artifact: Any object made by human hands, but especially simple and primitive tools.

Beehives: Small stone chambers made by ancient man, mainly Celtics of ancient times, using a cobbling effect to make them look like beehives.

Bronze Age: A period of human culture characterized by the use of bronze tools and weapons, around 3,500 to 1,000 B.C. It came after the Stone Age but before the Iron Age.

Cairn: A conical heap of stones, built as a monument or landmark.

Carbon-dating: An intricate procedure which establishes the approximate age of carbon remains of archaeological specimens by measuring the amount of radioactive carbon-14 remaining in them.

Dolmen: A Neolithic tomb or monument consisting of a large stone laid across upright stones. Scandinavians called them "cromlechs."

Epigraphy: The study of deciphering, interpreting, and classifying ancient inscriptions.

Linear: Of, or relating to, a line or lines. Ogam and rune markings on stones are usually linear.

Manitou: Or god stone; a standing stone of ritual importance to Native Americans.

Megalith: From the Greek meaning large stone, used in Neolithic monuments in the construction work of ancient peoples.

Monolith: A large single-standing stone.

Neolithic: Of the Old World culture, thousands of years before Christ. The period of the development of settled agriculture.

Ogam (Ogham):   An alphabetical system of writing developed centuries ago in which the letters are represented by various combinations of lines or notches.

Oratories: Small chapels of stone for private prayer.

Petroglyph: A rock carving or stone picture.

Rune:	An angular script for carving on wood or stone, inscribed or written in Germanic languages: Old Norse, Finnish, or Scandinavian.
Runestone:	Runes inscribed in rock.
Souterrain:	Man-made underground tunnels and chambers.
Stonehenge:	A circular arrangement of pre-historic megaliths on Salisbury Plain, England, probably set up in the Neolithic/Bronze Age as an astronomical calendar.

Uncovered in the bedrock at Searsmount, Maine was this Celtic head adorned with carved acorn and oak leaves which are the holy objects of Druids. The head is now on display at Sturbridge Village Museum in Sturbridge, Massachusetts.

Photo by Malcolm Pearson.

At the north end of the island park on Commonwealth Avenue, Boston, sits noted historian Samuel Eliot Morison on a rock. At the south end, about a half mile away, standing on a pedestal is Norseman Leif Ericson, thought to be a visitor here in the year 1000 A.D. Morison insisted that Ericson was never in New England. Therefore, the park designer rightly separated them and placed them back to back, as far away from each other as possible.

The controversial Bourne Stone, once the threshold of an Indian church at Cape Cod. Epigrapher Dr. Barry Fell recognized the inscription on the stone as Celtic-Iberic and translated it to read: "Hanno takes possession of this place." Hanno was a noted explorer from Carthage who voyaged into the Atlantic in 425 B.C.

I
New Raiders of the Lost Ark

Into the computer age of the 1990s and beyond into the 21st century, the archaeological world of uncovering the hidden past of our ancestors is progressing by leaps and bounds. What was considered to be an improbability or even an impossibility fifty years ago, is accepted as fact in many scientific circles today. The theory of the drifting continents, which would have made professors as well as school children chuckle up their sleeves in the 1950s, is now an unquestionable fact - the continents were once one central mass that split apart and drifted - in fact, still continue to drift - into the continents we know today. The historical and archaeological worlds are also experiencing renewed inspection and reversals concerning old chestnuts of supposed indisputable fact. *"No evidence from the classic writers justifies the assumption that the ancients communicated with America,"* wrote noted historian Justin Winsor in 1889. *"Nor has anyone since discovered any such evidence,"* wrote leading historian Samuel Eliot Morison in 1971, in his *"The European Discovery of America."* At the time, Winsor was probably right, but Morison, if he had personally researched further into archaeological discoveries being made and reported on during his lifetime, might not have been so definite. Morison, however, mocked writers, historians, teachers, and archaeologists who presumed that any white man touched American soil before Columbus. Being a frustrated poet as well, he caustically summarized his feelings in one of his poems with: *"So, now you know, unless you're a fool, that they told you all wrong, when you studied at school."* Unfortunately, Morison's elite followers, wearing blinders provided by him, follow in his footsteps today and dare not venture into this new age of ancient discovery. Yes, Samuel, it's safe to say that what they told us at school is wrong, not all of it, but quite a bit. Not to do this revered Harvard historian an injustice, much evidence on early European settlement in America has been uncovered since his book, *"The Northern Voyages,"* was published in 1971. Yet, some of the evidence was available then, and he was critical without investigating it. He, in fact, was belittling the discoverers, some of them being fellow historians and scientists from Harvard — colleagues, if you will.

Probably the most prominent of the *"mavericks"* who disrupted and continues to disrupt Morison's conservative followers (Morison died in 1976) is Harvard professor emeritus Barry Fell. Fell, a distinguished epigrapher, wrote the books *"America B.C."* and *"Saga America"* which began to quench what Fell calls, *"an overwhelming thirst for historical information."* Since Samuel Eliot Morison enough time has gone by, *"and with this passage has come a shift of opinion,"* says Barry Fell. *"Already a number of American historians accept the reality of Norse voyages in the eleventh century, and some admit to even earlier voyages."* One of Fell's theories, backed by intriguing evidence, is that parts of America, including New England, were settled before the Viking explorations of about 1000 A.D. This was apparently accomplished by Phoenicians and Iberian-Celts hundreds of years before the coming of Christ. The Phoenicians were renowned seamen and traders of the ancient world. Chroniclers of the time wrote that they not only ventured well beyond the *"Pillars of Hercules,"* meaning Gibraltar, and traveled the Atlantic Ocean with ease, but as Greek historian Herodotus in 5 B.C. wrote, *"The Phoenicians could sail for thousands of miles without falling off the edge of the earth."* The Iberian-Celts and Phoenicians traded and intermarried, and both used *"ogam,"* the language of horizontal and vertical lines engraved in stones recently found and deciphered in New England. The Iberian-Celts, like the Phoenicians, came out of North Africa and settled in what is now part of Portugal and Spain (Iberia) for some 200 years. They then sailed on en-mass to settle Erin, *"the furthest island west,"* which they renamed after their King Milisious's son, Ir — *"Irland."* The neighboring island they named for the King's wife, Scotia — *"Scotland."* This was all some 100 years before the coming of Christ. Barry Fell and some others archaeologists and historians now claim that these same ancestors of the Irish and Scots were coming here to New England possibly as early as 500 B.C.

When Barry Fell first began to decipher and report on these Iberic and ogam inscriptions found throughout coastal America, including all of New England, few scholars took notice. Then, beginning in the early 1970s, there came criticisms, but as Fell reports, *"one by one, competent scholars who hold responsible positions in universities and museums are coming forward with confirmations of the decipherments. At first the confirmations were made by linguists in Europe, North Africa, and the Middle East, and were published in technical papers that they wrote. Later confirmation was reported from American scholars."*

The great King Solomon hired Phoenicians to sail to India to bring him gold, silver, and ivory. Herodotus also reveals that the Egyptian Pharaoh Necho hired Phoenicians from Carthage to sail around the continent of Africa in 600 B.C. Their three-decked 80-foot galleys made it from the Red Sea into the Indian and Atlantic oceans, ending up in the Canary Islands, thence back to Egypt. When they returned after their three years voyage, the Phoenician mariners claimed that, when sailing around the continent, the sun shone on their right side and not on the left. Neither the Pharaoh nor Herodotus believed them, but today scholars realize that they had indeed sailed beyond the Tropic of Capricorn and around the Cape of Good Hope, where, south of the equator, the sun crosses the sky in the north. There is further evidence that they may have sailed further than the Canaries, probably to the Azores, where many Carthaginian coins of the 4th century B.C. have been uncovered. A New England voyage would have been less than half the distance of their cruise around Africa.

At a Brazilian plantation in 1872, a stone was uncovered with a strange inscription on it. Ladislau Netto, Director of the Brazilian National Museum, recognized the writing carved into the stone as Phoenician. It read in part: *"We are the sons of Canaan from Sidon...Commerce has placed us on this shore...in the eighteenth year of Hiram our king. We left Ezion-Geber on the Red Sea in ten vessels and voyaged around Ham (Africa). We were separated by a storm and so came here, 12 men and 3 women. May the gods favor us."* The inscription on the stone was, of course, disputed. Samuel Eliot Morison called it *"a transparent invention,"* but in 1968, the equally revered expert of ancient history, Cyrus H. Gordon of Brandeis University, declared it *"authentic Punic writings."* Many more Iberic and Phoenician stone carvings have been discovered in South America since then, especially in Brazil.

The Punic Wars (Carthaginian Phoenicians against Romans and Greeks) went from about 480 B.C. to 275 B.C., the Greeks finally destroying the city of Carthage. The Greeks and Romans then took power over the Phoenicians, outlawing their religious rituals, including human sacrifice. The Phoenicians sailed away from North Africa in great numbers, never to be seen again. Did they, like the Pilgrims of 1620, sail to the Americas to avoid religious persecution? The famous Greek philosopher Aristotle, in his *"Marvels of the World,"* written in 335 B.C. revealed that *"outside the pillars of Hercules, the Carthaginians have found an island having woods of all kinds, with remarkable fruit and navigable rivers. Some Carthaginians live there, and their chief will kill any who would come there."*

This *"island"* could be anywhere in the Atlantic, but it couldn't be part of Europe or the British Isles; the Greeks were aware that the Phoenicians were trading with Britain and other ports along the European coast. The Greek trader Pytheas secretly followed a Phoenician ship to England and the Shetlands at the end of 4th century B.C. to find out where they obtained amber and tin. Pytheas also traveled to *"Thule,"* which he said was a six day sail from the Shetlands. Many scholars believe that the mysterious Thule that Pytheas speaks of is Iceland, which supposedly wasn't discovered or settled until 700 A.D. by Irish Culdee monks. Some historians, geographers, anthropologists, and archaeologists today think the Pytheas' *"Thule"* may have been New England, Nova Scotia, or Newfoundland, which would have been some sixteen days sail from the Shetlands.

"After the fourth century B.C.," says Barry Fell, *"our visitors began to bring with them — and to leave behind — infallible date-markers that the mod-*

ern historian demands: those enduring metal discs called coins." It was another Harvard graduate, James Whittall of Rowley, Massachusetts, founder of the Early Sites Research Society, who brought to Fell's attention a letter from the Reverend Thaddeus Mason Harris to John Quincy Adams about an episode on the Cambridge-Malden Road in 1787. As the minister galloped by, workmen who were attempting to widen the road, *"with a pick axe, struck a horizontal flat stone buried beneath the surface. When the slab was cleared and prized up, it concealed over two quarts of little square pieces of copper and silver metal."* The find attracted many passersby, none of whom could even guess what the hundreds of little metal pieces were. The road workers invited the onlookers to gather up what they wanted of what were thought to be valueless trinkets, and everyone stuffed their pockets. Other caches of similar copper-silver pieces were later found in Lynn and Cape Ann, Massachusetts. No one, for over 200 years, paid attention to the wave-like lines etched into these metal pieces, until Jim Whittall showed one to Barry Fell. Fell recognized the writing on the coin as *"Kufic,"* an ancient form of Arabic, known to the Iberians and Phoenicians. They were valuable ancient coins from North Africa, but what were they doing in New England? Phoenician coins minted at Carthage in the early third century B.C. were recently found at Waterbury, Connecticut by Frederick Gastonguat. *"They all belong to the earliest issue of Carthage,"* says Fell. The coins displayed the Punic letters *"O, M, M, Q, N, I"* which signifies *"in camp,"* meaning that the coins were *"military issue intended for use as pay for mercenary Greek and Iberian soldiers in the Carthaginian army."* The coins display the head of a horse, the emblem of Carthage. This same horse-head symbol, carved in minia-ture out of a piece of limestone, was uncovered deep in the earth at North Salem, New York, near the Connecticut border. This discovery was not far from a crude stone chamber and a giant dolmen believed to be an ancient memorial erected by Phoenicians or Iberian-Celtics. Ten miles north of where this intricately carved horse-head was found, at Lake Carmel, are the remains of some sixty rock huts, often called rock chambers or *"beehives,"* that are scattered about the landscape. Some believe these *"huts"* were built by early settlers as root cellars to store food. However, many archaeologists and historians have concluded, because of their unique old world construction and their mention of Indian oral history, that they are ancient dwellings of visitors from across the ocean.

A ceramic lamp was purchased by Norman Totten of Bentley College in 1980 from a New Hampshire antique dealer. When Norman asked about the his-tory of the lamp, he was told that it had been dug up at an Indian site in 1948 on Elm Street in Manchester, New Hampshire. Norman is an expert on ancient lamps, and he immediately recognized this one as being a wheel-made Mediterranean olive oil burning lamp of the late 3rd century B.C. What was such an ancient Old World lamp doing in the custody of New Hampshire Indians? At Concord, New Hampshire, in 1870, while digging to lay the foundation for the

Concord railway station, Lyman Fellows, one of my wife's ancestors, uncovered an ancient Iberian iron short sword with a decayed wooden knob hilt. The blade was remarkably preserved, and deeply etched down the length of this dagger-like weapon was ancient Iberian script. Barry Fell deciphered it to read: *"Hand wrought death dealing steel, able to cut through armor."* This ancient Celtic artifact was recently on display at Jamestown, Virginia in an exhibit of pre-Columbus artifacts uncovered in America.

Only four years before this Celtic sword was found underground, a *"mystery stone"* was dug up from under three feet of earth at Lake Winnipeasaukee, New Hampshire. Seneca Ladd of Concord, New Hampshire spied the oval object, a greenish stone with deep carvings on it, as workmen were digging a ditch along the shoreline. The stone was only eight inches by four inches, and weighed a mere 18 ounces, but it had a tapering hole bored right through it from top to bottom, and displayed a sleeping face and ten different intricate designs. Chiseled into the egg-like object was an ear of corn, the kernels exposed, with a bird, bear's paw, and deer's leg carved below it. It also had an eight-point star, a sun, and four arrows crossed to make the letter *"M."* The face with the closed eyes does not have Indian features and could be African, with a broad nose and thick lips. Experts in Indian art at the Smithsonian Institute in Washington, D.C. studied the stone egg and determined that it was not Indian. It is now in the possession of the New Hampshire Historical Society.

When Barry Fell was written up in Newsweek after discovering ancient Old World inscriptions in Pennsylvania in the mid-1970s, Jim Whittall, who had never met the Harvard professor, called him at his home in Arlington, Massachusetts. *"I've got a lot of New England stuff with inscriptions on them which I've collected over the years,"* he told Fell, a master at interpreting ancient inscriptions, *"and I'd like you to decipher them for me some time."* Fell invited him to come to Arlington, some thirty miles away, with his stuff *"immediately"* — and a great new friendship was born. It was to Bourne on the Cape Cod Canal that they took their first field trip together, where the famous *"Bourne Stone"* resides. It was discovered in 1658, a 3 1/2 foot by 18 inch slab being used as a threshold as an Indian church and was later moved to the nearby Aptuxcet trading post. On the underside of the stone was an inscription. All scholars and historians who had studied it, from the 17th century on, concluded that it was either ancient writing (Norse, Celtic, or Indian) or meaningless graffiti, possibly carved into the rock as a hoax. Harvard's Samuel Eliot Morison and Yale historian Robert Lopez would not accept it as authentic, but this was before Barry Fell took a look at it. Fell determined that the writing on it is ancient Phoenician, but he could not immediately determine what the message was. Two days after seeing the stone and recording the message, he called Whittall at 2 a.m., waking him from a sound sleep. *"It's Iberic,"* he shouted over the phone, and it reads:

"Hanno takes possession of this place." Fell's interpretation of the Bourne Stone sent out new waves of unrest and dispute throughout the parochial world of archaeologists and ancient historians, for Hanno was a merchant mariner from Carthage who sailed off seeking new lands from the west coast of Africa in 425 B.C.

The most controversial inscribed rock on New England is Dighton Rock at Berkeley, Massachusetts, on the Taunton River. As early as 1677, scholars such as Cotton Mather, Dean Berkeley, and Ezra Stiles have tried to decipher the messages chiseled into its ten foot by four foot sandstone face. Stiles was convinced that the rock was covered with ancient Phoenician petroglyphs. Mather sent drawings of the markings to the Royal Society of London to see what they thought, but the English scientists were non-committal. In 1837, Danish scholar Carl Rafn read Roman numerals and the name *"Thorfinn Karlsefni"* in the stone. Thorfinn supposedly sailed to America from Greenland in the year 1010. In this century, Brown University professor Edmund Burke Delabarre deciphered part of the inscription on the rock to read: *"Miguel Cortereal by will of God, here Chief of the Indians,"* along with the date 1511 and a Portuguese coat-of-arms. Miguel Cortereal, a Portuguese navigator, did disappear in 1501 with his crew, sailing the Atlantic in search of his explorer brother Gaspar Cortereal, who had also disappeared with his three ships and crews the year before. Their father, Joao Vas Cortereal, traveled to *"the land of the cod,"* thought to be Newfoundland in 1472, twenty years before Columbus' voyage.

"Dighton Rock is like the rocks you see along the highways, filled with graffiti," says Jim Whittall. *"It's where everyone wanted to leave a message. and it's the first stone in America that anyone paid any attention to. It was a bulletin-board for ancients, Native Americans, and colonials alike."* The rock with the mysterious hieroglyphs was moved to dry land a few years ago by the Commonwealth of Massachusetts and a building was built around it to preserve the inscriptions. Winter ice and constant submergence at high tide under the Taunton River, began obliterating some of the older markings. Also, in case one of the great scholars who deciphered the stone over the past 300 plus years is right, it's best to preserve what may be a most important piece of history. Even if the hodgepodge of scratches and scribblings can't ever be deciphered, Dighton Rock is a unique rock of ages. Sam Morison said, *"if the history of the Dighton Rock is nothing else, it is a remarkable demonstration of human credulity."* Right on, Sam!

About 125 miles north as the crow flies from Dighton Rock, another much smaller granite rock with an inscription was found in 1938 by Miss Frances Healey near her home at Hampton Falls, New Hampshire. Olaf Stranwald, a Washington runologist, visited Miss Healey to study the stone and search the headwaters of the Hampton River for Norse artifacts. Professor Stranwald was convinced that the inscription carved into the little stone was runic — a message from the Vikings, but he could not translate the brief message. At the time, Stranwald was unaware that the Norse markings and Celtic ogam writings were quite similar, and often mistaken by scholars, one for the other. It wasn't until 1975, when Jim Whittall showed a photograph of the *"Healey Stone"* to Barry Fell and epigrapher Donal Buchanan that the markings were identified as Libyan script. At first, these experts of the Epigraphic Society could not at first decode the message. Three years later, as Whittall was researching pre-Roman measurements and tables used by the Iberian-Celts, he discovered markings that were similar to those on the Healey Stone. He immediately called Fell and asked, *"Could the stone have been a measuring device, and could the script possibly have anything to do with measurements?"* A week later, Barry called Jim. *"How much does the stone weigh?"* he asked. Jim thought it a strange question, but he found out the weight of the stone and called back Barry Fell, who was then in California. Before Jim could say anything, Barry said, *"Jim, I bet you that you're going to tell me the stone weighs between 32 and 34 pounds."* *"It weighs 33 pounds,"* Whittall responded. *"Wonderful!"* exclaimed Fell. *"You've solved the puzzle — the message on the stone reads 'Certified to the Tunisian Standard.'* " The Tunisian 'Kula' was a lithic measure for standard weight of 33.35 pounds and Tunis, a North African-Mediterranean seaport, was near the ancient site of Carthage. Here was another new piece of evidence that Carthaginian Phoenicians came to America and explored this river in New Hampshire.

Further up the Atlantic coast on a narrow island located off the Damriscotta River in Maine, a Dr. Cushman of Wiscasset made an interesting discovery in 1851: *"As I was lifting the covering of shallow soil,"* writes the doctor in his journal, *"a smooth rock appeared, whereon the washing of the sea had laid bare numerous inscriptions in writing cut by human art in characters from one to four inches long, one-eighth of an inch deep, and covering the surface of ten feet."* The Indians had given the island its name, *"Damascotta,"* now Damiscove, supposedly meaning *"fishing place."* White fishermen of Europe had camped and fished here as early as the mid-1500s. Sketches of the markings discovered by Dr. Cushman were passed on to Barry Fell by Jim Whittall for identification and translation. Like the Healey Stone, Fell recognized the markings as ancient North African or Phoenician script, carved into the rocks prior to the birth of Christ. Two other messages, Fell explains, were warnings carved into the rocks for friends who supposedly would be coming to the island. Chiseled deep into the seaside stone, it read: *"Dama is waterless."* The message beside it, gouged out in Libyan script, read, *"Dama lacks water, the spring is blocked."* Fell dates these messages by the form of script as being about 2,300 years old. Dr. Barry Fell was also called out to Monhegan Island, Maine, by local anthropologists to decipher an inscription on another large seaside boulder. The strange writing, Fell concluded, is Iberian-Celtic, and reads *"Cargo platforms for ships from Phoenicia."*

All these messages are visible to people traveling by boat, as are two other Maine sites that are *"Bulletin Boards"* as Whittall calls them. They are covered with petroglyphs from ancient times right up to modern day, with the last chiseled symbols in the rocks being a heart and a final inscription, *"John loves Mary."* Both sites are whale back rocks, jutting out into the sea at Machiasport and at the Kennebec River in Embden. Even with such a jumble of messages carved into the rocks over the centuries, *"like all true petroglyphs,"* says Whittall, *"you wouldn't even know they were there at high noon under the direct sunlight, but just after dawn or just before sunset, they show up clearly. The older petroglyphs at both sites parallel those of Norway and Sweden,"* says Whittall, *"which indicates a probable intercourse between Native Americans and the Norse."*

The most puzzling of Maine's seaside rock inscriptions is at York Harbor. Somewhat eroded, it is large and ledgible overlooking the Atlantic Ocean. It is in ancient Latin and reads, *"There is a foam-decked rock far out at sea opposite the shore, which is covered by the waves in rough weather."* Jim Whittall, Barry Fell, and Early Sites photographer Malcolm Pearson visited the site to take molds of the inscription, which Fell concluded has *"the peculiarities of Iberian-Roman script."* Fell dates the inscription to 300-400 A.D. *"No lovesick Latin student could have done this,"* says Whittall, *"not just because it would have taken many days of hard labor to accomplish, but because no Latin student or professor of Latin for that matter, could know the Iberian style, for it was only recently revealed from newly discovered Roman ruins in Iberia."* Although the inscribed statement is copied from Virgil's Aenid Book, which might make it suspect, the great poet lived from 70 to 19 B.C., and the students of his work often repeated phrases from the book. Besides, there really is a foam-decked rock directly out to sea from York, Maine, called Boon Island Ledge, which is covered by waves in rough weather, and where many a ship and seaman have disappeared.

Two boys, playing on Great Chebeague Island in Casco Bay, in September of 1941, began scraping layers of moss from a large boulder facing the sea. To their surprise they uncovered a life-sized face carved with great care. Fishermen who had lived on the island in the 18th century had reported a carved face in the rocks, which they said had been discovered by the first island settlers. No one, however, could ever relocate the stone face until the boys stripped the layers of moss. After going to the island and studying the carving, Jim Whittall, who is an artist in his own right, concluded that, *"the Chebeague face was carved by a Celtic explorer, sometime before 1000 A.D. The artistic style of the carving is similar to that of Celtic artwork."* Another Celtic head, adorned with oak-leaves and acorns, was found years ago in the bedrock at Searsmount, Maine and is presently on display at Sturbridge Village Museum in Massachusetts. The connection to the oak is significant in this ancient carving. As the Pagan Celtic Druids considered the oak to be sacred, and the acorn and leaves were used in their religious rituals.

Probably the strangest and most controversial sculptured head ever found in New England was the granite oval uncovered under ten feet of soil in a newly-dug cellar-hole in 1810 at Essex, Massachusetts. It was twice life size, with ears, Roman nose, and deep set eyes. Because it looked like a piece of Roman sculpture, it was immediately dubbed *"The Roman Head,"* but no one could begin to guess who carved it, or what it was doing ten feet underground near the salt marshes of Essex. Owner of the land, Tom Burnham, placed the head on his gatepost for all who passed his new house to see. To attract further attention, he painted the head pink with red lips. In the winter months, he'd wrap a scarf around its jaw and plunk a top hat on its stone baldness. The head didn't move until 1825, when Burnham opened a bookstore in Boston and the head was displayed in the store window. By this time, the red and pink paint had chipped and worn off. Another store owner, seeing that the head attracted customers to Burnham's store, persuaded him to sell it for $200. An antique collector then bought it for an untold amount from this second store owner, and the next time *"Old Stone Head,"* as Bostonians called it, was seen again, was at the National Museum of Denmark. An Essex seaman who remembered the head on Burnham's gatepost asked the curator of the museum if this could be the same head. The few remaining flecks of pink paint brought them to realize that it was. The museum directors believed that they has been the victims of fraud, so they sold the head to the Essex seaman, and he brought it back home to the North Shore of Massachusetts. He presented it to the Peabody Museum in Salem, where it remains to this day. Jim Whittall believes that the controversial head is Celtic, and probably ancient.

It seems, the Romans, however, did visit our shores, and Barry Fell believes there is enough evidence to place them here, probably as traders with the Indians, from about 100 B.C. to 400 A.D. By this time in ancient history, Rome had conquered many lands, including the Iberian Peninsula, and as the message on the rocks at York, Maine indicates, these were Iberian-Romans. The Celts had left Iberia in this time frame and had settled in Ireland and Scotland, and possibly in New England as well.

At Ipswich, Massachusetts, originally an Indian village called Agawam, many Indian artifacts have been uncovered over the years. Two ancient Roman spoons were dug up in the 1800s from an Indian grave near where Ipswich High

- 13 -

School stands today, and a Roman coin with Iberian script on it and a hole in the middle was found nearby. Archaeologist Warren Morehead went wild with anguish in 1930 after inspecting fragments of pottery found at an Indian shell heap at Ipswich, as he never could relocate the site. Morehead had determined that the pottery was not Indian at all, but Iberian ware.

At nearby Plum Island, overlooking Ipswich Bay, two young men, Al Locke and Sheldon Lane, were recently metal detecting after a severe storm. Locke passed his metal detector over a waterlogged piece of wood, obviously dredged up from the sea bottom. Surprisingly he got a reading. He dug his knife into the wood expecting to find an old nail or spike, but instead dug out a partially worn bronze coin, about the size of a silver dollar. Also found in the wood were two bronze ship's spikes about six inches long. Chris Ritter of Maine, a collector of Roman artifacts and a friend of the young men, identified the coin as a Roman Setterii. Embossed on the coin was the portrait of Emperor Severus Alexander, who was murdered at Mainz in 235 A.D. Peter Pratt, a coin dealer of nearby Georgetown, Massachusetts, upon reading of the find by Locke and Sheldon in the newspaper, revealed that he, too, had found a Roman coin metal detecting in the same area at Plum Island in 1974. It was also a bronze Setterii of the 3rd century A.D. Plum Island, by the way, is only a few miles from Essex, Massachusetts, where the Roman Head was uncovered in 1810, and less that twenty miles from York, Maine and the Roman-Iberic Latin message about treacherous Boon Island. Only a few miles down the North Shore from Ipswich and Essex, four fourth century Roman coins were recently found clustered together under the sand at Dane Street Beach, Beverly. A Roman coin depicting Septimus Severus, who ruled Rome from 193 to 211 A.D. was plowed up at Grafton, Massachusetts by Mrs. Curtis Robie, and another, dating to 80 A.D., was uncovered near the Persumpscot River at Wesbrook, Maine. Two more were recently dug up using a metal detector at Bethel, Vermont. These were minted at Rome in 72 A.D. Surely, there are many more Roman coins that have been found and either not identified or not reported. One must ask, how did they get here?

Archaeologist Frank Glynn was presented with a big box full of Indian artifacts by a boy in Clinton, Connecticut, which had been uncovered while digging an Indian shell heap over a period of four years. Included in the box was what the boy thought was an Indian pipe, but Glynn recognized it as an ancient oil lamp, typical of the Mediterranean area. Frank shipped the lamp off to his learned colleague and noted English archaeologist T. C. Lethbridge at Cambridge University. A few British archaeologists inspected the lamp and concluded it was late Roman of the eastern Mediterranean, designed between 700 and 800 A.D. Glynn, who died in 1968, was afraid to show it to American archaeologists, for fear they would laugh at his and his British colleagues' conclusion. Only within the last few years would members of the archaeological world consider an

Rölvaag

~~Ole Edar~~

OLE   Edvart

1876-1931

Giants in the Earth

ancient Roman lamp found in an American Indian campsite as conceivably feasible. Like the ancient olive oil lamp dug up at the old Indian camp in Manchester, New Hampshire, it strongly suggests that New England Indians were trading with Romans or with peoples the Romans had conquered.

Another important puzzle piece to this ancient mystery of trade between Phoenicians, Iberian-Celts, Iberian-Romans, and Indians was recently brought to light by scuba diver Norwood Bakeman, who spends much of his spare time combing the muddy sea bottom of Castine Bay, Maine for Revolutionary War relics. One day, Norman stumbled upon something much older: two large ceramic jars. He hauled them ashore, but nobody seemed to know what they were or how old they might be, until Jim Whittall, hearing of the find, ventured up to Maine to take a peek at them. *"Not only are they probably ancient,"* says Whittall, *"but in all probability they come from the Iberian Peninsula, where they are called 'Spanish olive jars.' Marks around the edges of these Castine anforeta show wear from constant chafing, caused by the rolling of the vessel on long journeys at sea while the jars were secured by lines to the deck or in the hold."*

Another of these Punic type jars, used to haul olives, liquids, and other loose items in ancient times, were dragged up from 120 foot depths in nets by a Newburyport fisherman in 1991, and two more were dug up in Boston proper; one during construction of the underground garage at Boston Common. Another was pulled out of deep muck as workmen widened the Southeast Expressway; others were found at Castine and Jonesboro, Maine. What are all these ancient anforeta jars doing here? If the ancients didn't come to our shores to explore and trade, what is all their stuff doing here? And why are messages being found carved into rocks that face the sea and river mouths in their languages? Some hard-line archaeologists and ancient scholars remain unconvinced, whereas others, even though noncommittal, are remaining flexible. The evidence presented here thus far is not irrefutable, but it certainly is convincing. As Jim Whittall says, *"Archaeology is not a hard science, even though many mainstream academics may think it is. It's a life-long dedication to study and probing with an open mind and a willingness to dare — it's a search for the truth, and when the truth reveals changes our thinking 180 degrees, it's then that the truth hurts, and we must bare the pain, hopefully without a whimper."*

"When I was a young man," adds Whittall, *"my stepfather would sometimes bring me to the exclusive Somerset Club in Boston for lunch, and Samuel Eliot Morison was often there. I asked my stepfather to introduce me to the great historian, and he did. Upon visiting his table, I asked him, 'What of this wonderful ancient village recently uncovered in Salem, New Hampshire, called Mystery Hill?' 'My young man,' he replied, 'you obviously won't succeed in the*

field you're pursuing by asking questions like that.' Morison was wrong, for it is by having an interest in such finds, no matter how unorthodox, and by asking questions about any and all discoveries, no matter how seemingly insignificant, that one succeeds in the archaeological field. " Jim Whittall is certainly a good example of that. Morison didn't dissuade him one bit.

A granite head was uncovered in 1810 at Essex, Massachusetts by Tom Burnham while digging a cellar hole. Because of its Roman nose, it was called "The Roman Head," but today, it is thought to be an ancient Celtic carving.

Photo by Alton Hall Blackington.

A large carved rock inscription in Iberic-Roman script (lower left) looks out to sea at York Harbor, Maine. Epigrapher Barry Fell (right) here working at the site, dates the inscription to 300-400 A.D.

Dighton Rock on the Taunton River is where, it seems, every early visitor and explorer to New England has left his mark. Cotton Mather, Puritan religious leader here in the 1600s, copied the inscriptions and shipped them off to the Royal Society in London in hopes that they might decipher them. We're all still waiting for their answer.

Photo by Malcolm Pearson.

Scuba diver Norwood Bakeman with ancient anforeta jugs he found on the sea bottom at Castine Harbor, Maine. Others have been dug up in Boston and pulled up in nets from the sea off Gloucester, Massachusetts.
Photo by Malcolm Pearson.

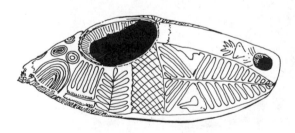

A Roman oil lamp (above) discovered by Frank Glynn of Connecticut, and a Mediterranean ceramic olive oil lamp (right) uncovered at an Indian site in Manchester, New Hampshire, which dates back to the 3rd century B.C. How did American Indians come to possess ancient lamps from the Old World?
Sketch by Gerturde Johnson. Photo by Norman Totten.

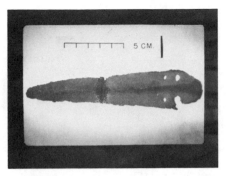

Four ancient coins depicting four Roman emperors of the 4th century B.C. were uncovered with a metal detector at Dane Street Beach, Beverly, Massachusetts.

This Bronze Age Celtic dagger was found in an Indian shell heap in 1900 at Merrimac Port, near Amesbury, Massachusetts.

The Healey Stone, found by Frances Healey at Hampton Falls, New Hampshire in 1938. Professor Olaf Stranwald of Washington claims that the stone has a runic message carved into it from Greenland Vikings who were visiting New England in the 11th century A.D. Barry Fell proved differently.

An egg-shaped stone with an ear of corn, deer's leg, bear's paw, a bird, eight-pointed star, the sun, four arrows, and a closed eyed face carved into it, was found under three feet of earth on the shore of Lake Winnipeasaukee, New Hampshire in 1866.

Photos courtesy of Early Sites Research Society, Rowley, MA.

Life sized stone face carved in ancient Celtic style (left) was uncovered under layers of seamoss at Great Chebeague Island, Casco Bay, Maine. It was discovered by the first white island settlers. Similar Celtic heads (right) are found on ancient gravestones in Ireland.

Ogam script of ancient Celtics is found carved deeply into stone throughout New England. Here is script recently found and chalked at Hampton, Connecticut.

(Top) "An ancient bulletin board," as Jim Whittall calls it, at Machias, Maine. There is also a similar one on the Kennebec River in Embden, Maine. Here Indians, European visitors, and others have left graffiti over the centuries. (Lower left) Whittall, with a team from the Early Sites Research Society, uses aluminum foil to enhance the petroglyphs for photographs. (Right) The Ancient Celtic ogam inscription at Monhegan Island, Maine, was deciphered by Dr. Barry Fell to read: "Cargo platforms for ships from Phoenicia."

II
Temples to the Sun

Jim Whittall spent much of his youth trampling through Europe and North Africa in search of ancient dolmens, stone chambers, temples, and tombs. He also spent many hours, as he still does, scouring the dusty shelves of libraries and museum research rooms to gain further insight into New England's marvelous ancient megaliths and the meanings of man-made structures and carved messages left behind by our ancestors. It was a day in May, 1983, while Whittall mused over the painting of a magnificent dolmen at the Peabody Museum in downtown Salem, Massachusetts (only a few miles from his Rowley home) that the usually once-in-a-lifetime flash of revelation filled his being. Jim was intrigued by dolmens and still is. He had seen quite a few of the giant rock structures made up of a heavy stone supported and balanced by three smaller stones set in a triangle in Europe, especially in England and Ireland. The Irish believe dolmens to be markers of the tombs of great chiefs and druid priests. The structures were erected by ancient man, and are considered a miraculous engineering feat. How did these men, without the assistance of proper tools, lift and balance boulders weighing from 30 to 90 tons squarely on top of three little boulders? And an even more pressing question is, why did they do it...just to mark the graves of chiefs and religious leaders?

"This is a nice looking dolmen," Jim commented to Mrs. Waterman the museum guide as he studied the large painting on the wall. She agreed. *"Where's it from...France, England, Ireland?"*

"None of the above," Mrs. Waterman smiled. *"It sits four miles down the road in Lynn."* Jim felt his skin tingle. *"I don't believe it,"* he shouted. *"I've traveled the world looking for these, and there's one in my own back yard?"*

Whittall got directions from Mrs. Waterman and was out the museum door and on his way to Lynn, an industrial city bordering Salem. On the top of Prospect Hill he found what the locals call, *"Cannon Rock,"* a 65 to 70 ton stone perched on three small granite boulders, looking like a robust military cannon about to fire out over the horizon. Locals thought it was a glacial oddity, caused by earth erosion that left the large boulder suspended two feet off the ground by the smaller rocks. Whittall immediately recognized what it was: *"a manuscript left in stone by ancient mariners from Europe, proof that they came here thousands of years before Columbus."* He was, as he said, *"very impressed."* And what impressed him even more than its enormity was that, *"it seems to be erected with mathematical precision."* Of another dolmen discovered earlier in North

Salem, New York, also for many years thought by locals to be a glacial oddity, noted archaeologist Sal Trento concluded that it also *"seems to be erected with precision in the mathematical placement of supporting legs."*

Whittall soon discovered that the *"cannon"* at Prospect Hill is pointing at two other smaller dolmens located on nearby hilltops. That enticed him to search even further for ancient rock chambers, which often times are found in proximity of dolmens in Europe. Lynn was once the shoe capitol of the nation and Whittall soon decided that any and all beehive rock chambers, if they ever existed there, would probably have been destroyed by the building of brick shoe factories and three-decker homes. He did, however, remember talk of such a chamber at a seaside ledge outcropping in Nahant, Massachusetts only a couple of miles from the Lynn dolmens. This little rock structure, made up of large boulders capped with seven massive roof slabs, has long been called *"The Witch Cave."* It was here that an accused witch of Salem and her daughter hid to escape the hangman's noose in 1692. This rock chamber was known by America's first Puritan settlers, and there is possibly a connection between it and the Prospect Hill dolmen, but we'll probably never know for sure. When Jim Whittall showed the Lynn dolmens to Barry Fell, he commented that, *"I find it difficult to distinguish the North American examples from the European ones and believe that both sets were produced by ancient builders who shared a common culture."*

When Jim Whittall was Director of the Archaeological Department of N.E.A.R.A. (New England Antiquities Research Association) back in the 1970s, the existence of a dolmen at Martha's Vineyard came to the department's attention, and Jim went to the Vineyard to investigate. It is much smaller than the Prospect Hill dolmen, with larger supporting stones. He informed William Austin of Chilmark, Massachusetts, owner of the land where the dolmen stands, that *"the structure should date between 1,000 and 2,000 B.C. or older. I have obtained datings on similar stone structures here in New England of this time period, and I further feel that this structure should be added to the continuing evidence of Bronze Age European contact with North America."* Islander C.B. Johnson, while visiting Bohuslan on the Swedish coast shortly thereafter, informed Jim Whittall that he saw *"a dead ringer for the Chilmark cromlech (dolmen) with the same arrangement of stones. It's as old as the pyramids of Egypt - 3,000 to 2,500 B.C."*

In 1934, William Goodwin, a wealthy Hartford insurance executive who became obsessed with archaeology, was the first to investigate the Chilmark dolmen. It is on the western slope of a hill overlooking No Man's Land, a smaller island off the Vineyard. This is where runic Norse writing chiseled into rocks was discovered a few years later, but was thought to be a hoax. Goodwin cleared the brush and debris from the dolmen and measured the stones. There were three flat slabs, two placed perpendicular in the ground, and the third and largest, laid on top to form a table which one could sit under. Goodwin believed the dolmen marked a Viking grave. He dug inside the dolmen and found a fire pit, but this was before carbon-dating. He took measurements and photos of the dolmen, then called a *"cromlech,"* meaning stone tomb, and sent them to the director of the National Museum of Denmark in Copenhagen. The reply, received a few weeks later, was that it *"is undoubtedly a Norse burial marker, but the style of monument is earlier than the period which Leif Ericson made his famous voyages."* Although many archaeologists today believe that the Norsemen visited our shores and may have even temporarily settled here, few believe that the Norse constructed the dolmens. Barry Fell, for example, emphasizes the fact that *"we're on the same latitude as the Iberian Peninsula,"* and the architecture of the overlapping stone technique found in chambers, man-made caves, and other such structures in New England, seems to be of Celtic origin. We still really don't know who constructed dolmens, nor do we know why they went through such exhaustive efforts to lift such heavy stones. More dolmens have been uncovered at Salem, Bartlett, and Sullivan, New Hampshire, Brooklyn, Connecticut, and Foxboro and Westport, Massachusetts.

Jim Whittall was in for another shock only a few months after his Lynn dolmen discovery. A professor at the University of Lowell, Roger McLeod, mentioned to him that there was a cluster of monoliths on a hill at a place called LeBlanc Park in Lowell . So, one chilly February afternoon, Jim went *"driving up there to LeBlanc Park. I saw a sight I had not seen since my travels in the British Isles. Situated on a mound were weathered megalithic stones. I was filled with disbelief - it just couldn't be - someone was having fun with my senses. Western Europe, yes, but here in Massachusetts, no. The reality of the scene before me was difficult to focus on, the parallel with sites I had seen in Scotland and Ireland was astonishing."* Whittall was staring at a cluster of standing stones, like those of Salisbury Plain, England, called Stonehenge, thought to be set up by men of the Bronze Age between 2,500 - 1,500 B.C. There are ten stones, each weighing from five to ten tons, arranged in an egg-like oval. Whittall measured the mound on which they stand to be 112 feet long by 56 feet wide. One stone had been knocked over, and another had been moved from the circle and adorned with a brass plaque to become the memorial stone for the park. Otherwise, Jim surmised, the stones were where some unknown ancient had placed them. Would they then, Jim wondered, provide astronomical information as like the famous circle of stones at Stonehenge have for thousands of years?

The city fathers of Lowell were not impressed with the circle of stones at LeBlanc Park. The academic archaeologists of the Samuel Eliot Morison meld considered the standing stones a folly, a practical joke performed by Irish lads on the old Yankee farmers of Lowell in the early 1900's. The academics had convinced the politicians and businessmen of Lowell that the stones were not important and that a proposed highway could certainly pass through that area and disrupt the circle of stones without the archaeological or historical scholars of the world caring one bit. Whittall, however, and a few others of the *"maverick"* archaeological fringe were furious that a plan to destroy the standing stones was in the making. Researchers, historians and archaeologists such as Ronald Dalton, Virginia Ross, Richard Lynch and Jay Pendergast, started digging into the local archives in an attempt to possibly authenticate the stone circle and thereby save it. They discovered that the hill where the stones stand had been called *"Druid Hill"* from at least 1890, and prior to that it was called *"Bridget's Hill."* The hill was owned in Colonial times by a farmer named Varnum, and prior to that it was part of the Penacook Indian village on the Merrimac River, led by the greatest of New England medicine men, Chief Passaconaway. Could it have been this great Sachem or one of his ancestors that constructed the circle of stones? Whittall doesn't think so. *"It has been the opinion of academics for a long time that the Northeastern Woodland Indian did not construct in stone other than to make hand tools and hearths,"* he says, but then retorts that, *"research on Native Americans does provide information on large stone constructions such as the Queen's Fort in Rhode Island, stone forts of the Mohegans, Lockmere in New Hampshire, and numerous accounts of large stone piles."* However, Whittall is quick to add that *"the unique character of the site certainly suggests an intrusion from another cultural group."* Research archaeologist Jay Pendergast from the American Institute of Archaeological Research, who undertook an extensive investigation of the site, concluded that *"the site is a result of ancient diffusion with Celtic European connections."*

Whittall was anxious to take the investigation one step further into the realm of *"archaeoastronomy."* *"Initial impressions of those persons researching this site,"* says Whittall, *"led to the belief that the placement of the stones was not arbitrary and that there might be astronomical significance. The stones are oriented east and west, and bearings taken between some of the stones indicated the possibility that the site was used to observe certain solar events."*

Over a period of six months, Whittall and members of his Early Sites Research Society made field observations at sunsets on dates which have ancient Celtic and Norse pagan significance. The first observation was made on the Equinox of September 22nd. *"The sighting was made by gun sighting along the highest point on a western stone from the peak of the eastern -most stone."* reports Whittall. *"We lost the sun disk behind a tree cover in the last few minutes of its setting, but the alignment noted to that point did indicate the sun would set behind stone number four, as predicated it might. On November first we returned to the site, primarily because it was the ancient Celtic ritual day of Samhain, and we got a sighting from stone nine over stone six, and we had a setting alignment. At the Winter Solstice, observations were again made, gun sighting over the peak of stone one to stone ten, 112 feet away. The thrill of this observation is beyond words. Obviously, a Winter Solstice sunset was important at some point in time to an observer on that hillside, and the stones were set up to record it. It is no folly. The red disk slowly descended in a long arc towards the point on the needle-like monolith until the point split the disk in half right to its center. The sun disk then rolled down the right side of the stone and sank behind the horizon. It only took minutes to observe, but the memory of the event will linger in my mind for some time."*

Two more trips by the Early Sites team were made to Druid Hill for sightings on January sixth, the Celtic festival of light, and February second, the Pagan feast of Mother Earth for the return of the sun and the end of winter. In Ireland, it is the feast of Saint Bridget, which recalled to the researchers that the earliest known name of the hill, its origin lost to antiquity, was *"Bridget's Hill,"* possibly just a coincidence. Stone and sunset alignments were made on these special days of the ancient calendar as well. Like giant sundials, these standing stones at Lowell mark the seasons and special solar dates of pre-Christian times, and like Stonehenge in England, this has been going on for centuries. To the British, Stonehenge is a cherished ancient treasure. In Lowell, Massachusetts, *"Druid Hill"* it seems, is considered a valueless white elephant where teenagers are allowed to spray paint the standing stones, and nobody seems to care. The latest report from Dick Lynch of Early Sites is that, *"the standing stones on the mound had sprayed graffiti on them. One stone was tipped over, and this toppled stone has important astronomical alignments associated with it. It is feared that LeBlanc Park is being somewhat neglected and this significant stone may be removed as a hindrance."* Dick Lynch ends his report by saying, *"This, of course, would be tragic."*

Druid Hill is but half a mile from the Merrimac River that meanders from the mountains of New Hampshire through northeastern Massachusetts to Newburyport and the sea. Some fifteen miles from these standing stones, along a tributary of the Merrimac, is New England's most well-known yet most controversial ancient complex. It is called Mystery Hill, and more recently, *"America's Stonehenge,"* and it is located in North Salem, New Hampshire, just across the Massachusetts border. It was in 1936 that a minister from Methuen, Massachusetts mentioned the strange village of rock in a Boston Globe article. That year, Malcolm Pearson, a photographer from Upton, Massachusetts, who became interested in stone chambers when he found one in his backyard some eight years earlier, ventured up to Salem, New Hampshire to photograph the structures. Malcolm was truly impressed at finding some twenty acres of cobbled chambers, dolmens, standing stones and other megaliths, and he immediately recognized them as probably being part of and ancient village. Little did Malcolm Pearson realize the that he would some day own all of these structures at Mystery Hill.

The site was originally owned by Jonathan Pattee, who built his home there in 1823 and lived there until 1843. Pearson interviewed Pattee's great grand- daughter after visiting the site, and she stated that Pattee had moved much of the stone work and had sold a lot of it. Also, some ten years prior to Pearson's visit, tons of stones had been hauled away from the site by horse and wagon to build sewers and curb stones in Lawrence, Massachusetts. Yet some chambers and dolmens remained intact. That year, 1936, Malcolm Pearson, now in his eighties, and amateur archaeologist William Goodwin, a wealthy Hartford insurance man, then in his eighties, got together. To preserve what was left of Mystery Hill, Goodwin bought the twenty acres that it stood on, and Pearson placed a chain link fence around it with *"Keep Out"* signs. In closely studying the site, Pearson and Goodwin discovered over twenty stone structures...caves of stone, chambers with fireplaces and chimneys, and other huge megaliths, walls, and standing stones, weighing from 15 to 20 tons. Under it all they uncovered a man-made drain that prevented flooding of the complex. The center of the village was built on the sloping side of a hill, with a large courtyard of stone near the top. One of the most intriguing structures of all is called the *"oracle chamber."* It is the largest chamber on the site, shaped in a T. It has two standup passage ways, and inside on a wall is the carving of a running deer. There is also inside a cavern into which a small man might squeeze and hide, with a hole in the wall near a headrest. From here he can see out into the courtyard, and speak through a finely constructed stone tube called the *"oracle tube,"* allowing his voice to sound deep and unworldly to those standing in the courtyard or on the hill above. It was above this chamber near the mouth of the tube that Goodwin discovered a large ten-foot long slab weighing over four tons with a deeply and evenly chiseled groove along all four edges of it. Goodwin dubbed it *"the Sacrificial Table,"* and concluded it was used to sacrifice animals or humans to the gods in some type of Pagan ceremony. The tube, most surmise, was where some high priest hid himself and spoke to the gathered throng, as if his voice were coming from the table, with words of warning or wisdom from an underworld deity.

Goodwin had done a lot of prior archaeological work in the West Indies and at the Indian mounds in the Midwest. *"He was a tremendous research man,"* says Malcolm Pearson today, *"but he was a poor organizer."* Archaeological historian and writer Charles Boland states that *"Goodwin's energy may have destroyed some evidence, for his was not a professional dig."* Goodwin wrote a book on Mystery Hill in 1946 entitled, *"The Ruins of Great Ireland in New England,"* which truly made him an object of controversy. In his book, he concludes that Mystery Hill was once a Celtic monastery constructed by Irish Christian monks in the 10th century. Goodwin's theory seemed plausible, for there was a large group of monks called *"Culdees"* who were driven out of Ireland around 800 A.D. by the Vikings. These monks were converts from Pagan Druidism, and although they had discontinued human sacrifices, they often sacrificed animals to God in a ritual before eating them. The Culdees sailed their leather-skinned boats, called *"curaghs,"* to Iceland, but by 800 A.D. the Vikings came to Iceland to settle in, as Iceland's ancient historian Ari Thorgilsson wrote in 1026 A.D., *"the Culdees disappeared from Iceland in a night, leaving many of their religious articles behind them."* Thorgilsson also writes that when the Vikings under Eric the Red colonized Greenland in 1007 A.D., they found remnants of white cloth and many religious articles, presumably left behind by the Irish Culdee monks in their great haste to once again avoid the warring Norsemen. William Goodwin's contention is that they then came to New England, sailed up the Merrimac River to what is now Haverhill, Massachusetts, and settled on the high ground nearby at Salem, New Hampshire, which was once part of Haverhill. It was at Mystery Hill, Goodwin believed, these Culdee Monks converted many Indians to Christianity.

Dr. Hugh Hencken, Director of Prehistoric Studies at Harvard, visited the site with the intent to write a paper based on Goodwin's theory for the <u>New England Quarterly,</u> a publication edited by Samuel Eliot Morison. Although Hencken admitted similarities with beehive huts and soutterains, and standing stones found in Ireland and Britain, Dr. Hencken did not think the structures were built by Irish monks. In his article he stated that, *"the site deserves more than a merely negative conclusion,"* but he concluded that the buildings were erected by Colonials for vegetable cold storage. This, of course, infuriated Goodwin, and he was incensed even further when Morison would not publish his rebuttal to Hencken's conclusions. Morison then, in one of his popular books, rubbed salt in Goodwin's wounds by writing, *"Hugh Hencken, the Irish archaeologist, investigated the site and reported it to be unlike anything ever heard of in Ireland."* This was untrue. Malcolm Pearson, who escorted Hugh Hencken when he visited Mystery Hill, distinctly heard the doctor say, *"This is like the stone work I've been excavating in Ireland and England."* In fact, anyone who has been to Mystery Hill and to Sleigh Head on the Dingle Peninsula in Western Ireland would see a striking resemblance. Morison also concluded that *"the Sacrificial Stone has a gutter around the edge, supposedly to let a victim's blood run off; this, Hencken points out, was one of the lye-stones commonly used in New England to wash out lye from wood ashes."* Again, Morison misquotes Doctor Hencken, for he didn't say it was a lye-stone, he said it could be, but even the plausibility that it is a lye-stone is wrong. Lye-stones were usually much smaller and round, not rectangular. Someone would have to be a true glutton for labor to groove out the edges of a ten-foot lye-stone. Hencken might have been an archaeologist, but he seemingly knew little about Colonial America. As Malcolm Pearson points out, *"The colonists knew how to use stones, but they wouldn't make a structure that wasn't useful to them. They did make vegetable storage huts out of stone, but they followed a very finite pattern. The floor must be sandy to keep the interior dry, or the food will rot, and vegetable huts had to be ventilated, and have an opening big enough to back a wagon up to it for loading and unloading. It defies all rationale that the chambers at Mystery Hill be called vegetable storage huts."*

It was Doctor Hencken himself who made note of an ancient, large, decayed pine stump growing through the foundation of one of the chambers. The stump and original tree, which was later carbon dated to be well over 250 years old, were there before Mr. Pattee moved in in 1823, meaning that the chamber was there before Pattee too. This further refutes Hencken's conclusion, for before Mr. Pattee built there, Mystery Hill was a wilderness, and no Colonial stored his vegetables miles away from his farm. The first settlers came in 1730, 25 miles away from Mystery Hill.

Samuel Eliot Morison took one last swipe at William Goodwin, twenty years after Bill died. In 1970, Morison wrote, *"William B. Goodwin, an insurance executive of Hartford, Connecticut, spent a fortune following various archaeological will o' the wisps, including an alleged pre-Vinland or at least pre-Columbian 'Irish stone village' in North Salem, New Hampshire."* When Goodwin died, the *"will o' the wisp"* was, surprisingly, left to Malcolm Pearson in the old man's will. Even with the chain-link fence erected around it, Mystery Hill became a popular picnic ground, but as long as there was no destruction, Malcolm didn't discourage picnic goers from sneaking through the numerous holes in the fence. One picnicker was a young man named Bob Stone. On his first visit to Mystery Hill with his wife and another couple, he announced that, *"Some day I'm going to own this place."* Today, he does. He saved hard earned cash and first leased it and then bought it from Malcolm Pearson. He invited archaeologists and other scientists from various universities and societies to come investigate and even dig, if done in a professional manner. In 1958, he opened Mystery Hill to the public, and today he has renamed it *"America's Stonehenge."*

After some thirty-five years of intensive research and digging by a variety of experts, Bob Stone has concluded that *"William Goodwin had the right church, but the wrong pew."* Radio carbon testing of charcoal pits on the site provided dates from 173 B.C. and 2,000 B.C., which would certainly make both Goodwin and Morison turn over in their respective graves. This could, however, mean that ancient American Indians built Mystery Hill, but the construction certainly indicates European and Celtic.

Besides the carbon dating, the most exciting revelation for Bob Stone was when archaeoastronomers came to Mystery Hill to see if there could possibly be any astronomical alignments to the many standing stones lined up about the perimeter. On December 21 in 1970, the shortest day of the year, Bob and Brian Sullivan, his photographer, were there at sunset to capture this most southerly setting of the sun sitting perfectly on the tip of this largest south facing monolith. Crowds now gather there each year on December 21st to watch this dramatic sunset, as ancients did possibly thousands of years before. Slowly but surely, through the year, each important sunrise, sunset, and ancient holiday, like Halloween is recorded at the tips of various monoliths throughout the Mystery Hill site. Mystery Hill, then, is not a village. Bob Stone doesn't think anyone ever lived there, but the ancients would come there to worship, and to understand through their Druidistic leaders that there were seasons and holidays that could be timed to a date, and that there was a precise system to the earth and the stars, sun, and moon. Mystery Hill is a large Bronze Age calendar. *"A Neolithic temple,"* says Jim Whittall, *"a place of ceremonies."* Barry Fell believes there was a great Celtic community in New England and this was their church. But, even with the indisputable carbon dating and megalithic astronomical complex alignments, Harvard College still sponsors a course, taught by Professor Stephen Williams, in keeping with the Morison elitists, titled *"Fantastic Archaeology,"* in which they annually blast Bill Goodwin, and all others who believe anyone beat Columbus to the New World. Says Malcolm Pearson, *"There is man-made stone work in New England by a culture that was here and was not Indian. Obviously there were Europeans here at some time, evidently from 3,000 to 4,000 years ago. Our academics, the classic scholars, don't recognize this. Why not, I don't know. They will ask, 'Where are the artifacts?' Yet, there are tons of stone work that can't be explained. So, where are the artifacts? The academics can't lift them they're so heavy."*

Martha's Vineyard "cromlech."

"Cannon Rock Dolmen," Lynn, Massachusetts (upper left). Jim Mavor and Byron Dix at "Cat-faced Dolmen," North Salem, New York (upper right). "Table Dolmen," Westport, Massachusetts (below). "Hairy Dolmen" in Sligo, Ireland (bottom).

"Wedge chamber," also called the "Witch Cave" in Nahant, Massachusetts, where a woman accused of witchcraft hid out with her daughter in 1692. The chamber is thought to be of ancient vintage.
Early Sites photos.

Underground man-made chamber at "Turtle Mound" in Andover, Massachusetts, is also an ancient burial site.

Standing stones, Druid Hill, Lowell, Massachusetts.
Photo by Dick Lynch.

A typical ancient Celtic "Ring of Stones," (top) used by Pagan Druids and early Christians as a calendar, observatory, and religious ceremonial gathering place, usually found on the tops of hills in Europe. The ring below, however, is in Lowell, Massachusetts, its standing stones lining up perfectly for solstice sunset alignments and a host of Celtic Pagan feast days.

Photo by Dick Lynch.

William Goodwin, pictured here during his first visit to Mystery Hill, New Hampshire in 1936. He bought the twenty acres covered with chambers and other stone structures and fenced it in.
Photo by Malcolm Pearson.

Mystery Hill, North Salem, New Hampshire, as it looked when Goodwin bought it in 1936. Twenty stone caves and chambers were found within the compound.
Photos by Malcolm Pearson.

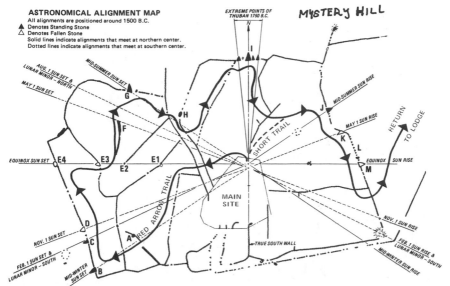

ASTRONOMICAL ALIGNMENT MAP
All alignments are positioned around 1500 B.C.
▲ Denotes Standing Stone
△ Denotes Fallen Stone
Solid lines indicate alignments that meet at northern center.
Dotted lines indicate alignments that meet at southern center.

EXTREME POINTS OF
THUBAN 1750 B.C.

MYSTERY HILL

(Top) is astronomical alignment of Mystery Hill standing stones and chambers to the sun, moon, and stars. It has recently been discovered that Mystery Hill, like Stonehenge in England, is a working observatory and centuries-old calendar. *(Below right)* is the Winter Solstice standing stone at Mystery Hill (see cover), where the sun sets into the peak of the rock on December 21st, the shortest day of the year. *(Below left)* is the sacrificial stone, found by William Goodwin, thought to be for animal and possibly human sacrifices.

Photos courtesy of Bob Stone.

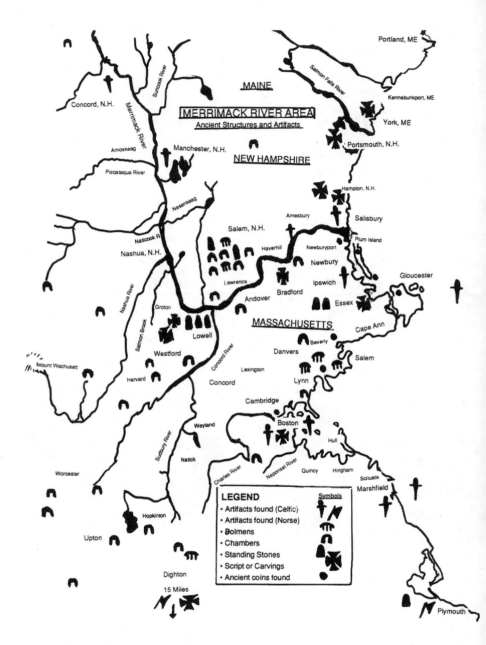

The Merrimac River area, a seemingly active avenue for ancient voyages and riverside settlements.

III
To the Promised Land

Those who lived in monastic settlements in Ireland, Scotland, and the outer islands lived in beehive dwellings, and unlike solitary monks, as we think of them today, those early monks were married and lived with their families. There were also female monks. Their worship was independent of the Catholic Church and was a blending of Christianity and Paganism. In fact, religious cults like the Culdees (Worshipers of God) also practiced ancient Druidism. Paganistic practices didn't cease in Ireland until the coming of Saint Patrick, and the Scots patron saint, Columba, in the mid sixth century A.D., was fond of saying *"Christ is my Druid."* Many of our religious holidays are actually offshoots of Pagan holidays. Easter, for example, from the goddess of Spring, *"Eostre,"* was celebrated for thousands of years before the coming of Christ, at the full moon following the vernal equinox. These monks wanted to keep track of these religious holidays annually, and so they developed their own unique calendars in stone.

In Ireland, Scotland and New England, thanks to the efforts of archaeoastronomers James Mavor, Byron Dix with Jim Whittall, many monastic sites have been examined and it has been determined that they are astronomically oriented. There are some 105 such chamber sites in Massachusetts, 51 in New Hampshire, 41 in Vermont, 62 in Connecticut, 12 in Rhode Island, and 4 in Maine. The largest drywall corbelled chamber site was uncovered in 1988 in Thompson, Connecticut by Dick Lynch. This circular beehive structure is 17.5 feet in diameter and ten feet high on the inside, with a six-foot entrance passage. It is similar to European beehives built in the Bronze Age. Nearby sits a 45 foot by 20 foot boat-shaped cairn. In visiting the chamber site, Jim Whittall noticed, *"Three boulders of exceptional size, the shape of triangles, have been placed up right in the wall. Since this feature was unusual, I suspected that they had some special significance. In Ireland, I have seen a similar arrangement in an ancient chamber at Carrowkeel in County Sligo and in the Medieval church wall at Killinagh in County Caven. This feature in the latter is said to be a tribute to the deity 'lug.' In Scotland at the monastic site of Eileach and Naoimh in the Garvellachs Islands this feature can be seen in the chapel wall and at a Culdee church off the West Coast of Ireland. Why, I ask, would such an arrangement be in a structure in New England, unless there is some connection in origin and time?"*

Connecticut's Thames River drainage area has an extensive collection of these ancient chambers with architectural features which parallel to an unusual degree chambers in Ireland and Northwestern Scotland. Radio-carbon dating at some of the chamber sites has shown activity well before the Colonial period.

"There are more unexplained rude stone monuments in Thompson, Connecticut," says Whittall, *"than elsewhere in New England."* Only three miles out of Stamford, Connecticut, there is a cluster of thirteen such drywall huts. They were long thought by the locals to be Indian dwellings, but in 1870 an old Stockbridge Indian named Joe returned to the site of his ancestors for a visit. His people had gone west after *"much wretchedness among my people"* while they were in Connecticut. Joe said that his ancestors had told his people that they had found three huts when they first arrived in Connecticut. They were not comfortable to his people, so they moved across the Ripowam to the high ground to live. Therefore, these stone huts were there before the Colonials came in the 1600s and before the Indians came. But then, who built them? At this writing they have been bulldozed away to make room for modern buildings.

Probably the most intriguing archaeological site in Connecticut is located in Groton and is called *"Gungywamp,"* thought to be an Indian name, but is actually ancient Gaelic meaning, *"Church of the people."*

Besides containing beehive chambers and petroglyphs, the Gungywamp site has a double circle of stones near its center, just north of two stone chambers. The spokesman for the Gungywamp Society, a group of some 500 people dedicated to preserving such sites in Connecticut, is David Barron. He led a group of archaeologists and students that recently uncovered two concentric circles of large quarried stones, 21 large slabs laid end to end at the center of the site. Barron doesn't dare speculate as to what the circles signify — a Druid's altar, an astronomical observatory, an old crushing mill? Extensive fire burning on some of the slabs was apparent, which led many to believe it was an ancient altar. Nearby there are several large pillar stones and one boulder slab that have been carefully positioned and supported in place, which persuaded some to believe it was an astronomical observatory. The Gungywamp site is only in the development stage archaeologically, and many feel there is much to be uncovered there. The research is ongoing, with over 200 interested groups visiting the site each year. Also recently discovered on the side of a cliff at Gungywamp were four heavily patinated symbols carved deeply into the rock. They are what is known as *"Chi-Rho,"* a series of holy signs popular in the 5th century A.D. to 1000 A.D. and found on Gaelic monuments. They look much like the letters *"R"* and *"P"* made into a cross with a loop or shepherd's crook at the top. Little Rean Whittall, Jim's daughter, made a remarkable discovery while they camped out for a week at the site. Some twenty feet from the trail, while playing archaeologist with her sister Heather, *"I found seven carved lines on a rock I was brushing off. I was not sure at first what they were, so I didn't tell my Dad. I didn't think he would consider them important. However, when I pointed them out to him, he thought otherwise."* The linear markings were ancient ogam, Rean had indeed made a remarkable discovery.

In the late afternoon of September 21st, while directing a team of diggers at the Gungywamp site, Dave Barron ducked into one of the chambers looking for a missing tool and got the surprise of a life. *"The setting sun had cast a beam of light through the vent shaft at the back of the chamber,"* said Barron. *"This beam of light slowly moved down the east wall and spotlighted into the small beehive crypt near the entrance. This stone-lined tube was designed precisely to permit the Equinoctial sunset to fully penetrate the chamber's dark interior only two days during the year. The beam of sunlight entering the small stone tube, illuminates the entrance of the hidden side chamber on the Equinox, March 22 and September 21. Both the upward angle and elevation of the light channel are precisely aligned to permit this illuminaire effect as seen in the ancient stone chambers in Europe. The high density of garnet in the stones appears to magnify the intensity of the sunlight entering the chamber. While observing the play of light through the tube on the Spring Equinox in 1989, I noted that there had been some modification to the light channel. At some point, after the construction of the tube, the base slab inside the chamber had been chiseled out to alter the passage of rays of sun. This would seem to indicate that the spotlighting effect didn't hit the intended target which was desired at first and a correction was necessary."*

"We don't know what the builder's intent was for this feature," says Whittall, *"but we do know that it certainly acts as a predictable calendar."* Vance Tiede of the Museum of Discovery in Bridgeport, Connecticut, is carrying out additional research at this Gungywamp chamber. This is to confirm other astronomical alignments of the sun on the solstices and cross quarter days, as well as moon rises and sets, correlating his work with known monastic calendar sites in Ireland and Scotland. The charcoal carbon-date at the circles of stones is about 600 A.D. Gungywamp certainly seems to be a Celtic monastery, similar to those found in the British Isles. But there are still doubters and much more research and archaeological investigation is needed.

At Montville, Connecticut, across Hunt's Brook, which is a drainage area of the Thames River, a giant man-made cave, called a *"souterrain"* by archaeologists, was discovered by accident after the 1938 hurricane. An old oak tree had been uprooted, dislodging two heavy capstones from the underground structure. To enter, one must squeeze into a two-foot by two-foot opening and then crawl 38 feet through a drywall passageway and then into a cobbled chamber. This souterrain is just across the brook from the Gungywamp complex. Located on the slope of a hill above and near this man-made cave are 100 rock cairns, great piles of various sized stones. Whittall reports, *"Some of these stone piles are crude; others are carefully constructed conical monuments. Whether the cairns have a direct relationship or not with the souterrain is unknown."*

Both Whittall and Dave Barron believe, however, that this complex is in some way connected with Gungywamp.

The 600 A.D. carbon-test date at Gungywamp fits perfectly into the travels of an Irish saint called Brendan. In *"Navgatio Sancti-Brendani,"* the book written about his adventures, Brendan says he was looking for *"God's Promised Land,"* and that *"God had left stepping stones to follow in order to find it."* Where Brendan got this information is lost to history, but he spent much of his life with his followers in pursuit of finding this special place. Possibly Brendan followed the symbolism of the Holy Bible, for in the Book of Joshua it says, *"When the whole nation had completed the crossing of Jordan (into the promised land) the Lord said to Joshua, 'Choose twelve men from the people, one from each tribe, and order them to take up to twelve stones from this place in the middle of Jordan, where the priests have taken their stand. They are to carry the stones across and place them in the camp where you spend the night' ... Joshua also erected twelve stones in the middle of the Jordan at the place where the priests who carried the Ark of the Covenant had stood; they are there to this day."*

It is pretty well determined today that Brendan and six fellow monks in a thirty-six foot skin-covered sailboat, used places like Scotland, the Hebrides, Iceland, Greenland, Labrador, Newfoundland, and Nova Scotia, as their stepping stones to find the Promised Land — New England. Leaving Dingle Bay, Ireland, about 585 A.D., he and his crew didn't return home for seven years. Brendan, The Navigator, called The Promised Land *"Saint Ailbe,"* and on the map Columbus used to relocate the New World in 1492, there was a large island located in the middle of the Atlantic Ocean titled *"Saint Brendan's Island."* Then, about 200 years later, the Irish Culdee Monks probably used this same *"stepping stone"* route to settle in New England. Sailor Tim Severin followed this same route, leaving Dingle in a 36' leather boat, its sail bearing the Celtic cross in 1976 just to prove that these boats could make it to America and back to Ireland. Severin also ended up in New England. Considering the winds and currents and the curve of the globe, Severin realized this northwesterly route to America from Ireland is the shortest and quickest route.

If it was the monks from Dingle who erected some of the 275 beehive chambers and drywall souterrains in New England, it is not such an unusual surprise, since the Dingle Bay Peninsula is crammed with similar ancient structures. British archaeologists have no problem in identifying them back to the Bronze Age and earlier in Ireland, but to suggest that the New England structures date back that far is tantamount to sacrilege to many American historians and archaeologists. Some, of course, still insist that these chambers are vegetable winter storage huts, which seems to defy all logic. Jim Whittall adds another twist to the chamber mystery with the following statement.

"Deep in the woods of Southbridge, Worcester County, Massachusetts, in a gulch, there is located the Morse Hill Chamber, which is constructed in an unusual design. The structure has a passageway over eight feet long leading into the chamber. But the interesting feature of the construction is that the chamber has been built off at an angle from the axis of the passageway. Architecturally, the roof construction has strong parallels with some others along the ancient trail network in southeastern New England — the Pearson Chamber in Upton and the Webster Chamber in Webster, Massachusetts, as well as the Rocky Brook Chamber in Thompson and the Wolfden Chamber in Chaplin, Connecticut all were constructed along ancient trails. The design would suggest a common engineering practice, perhaps even built under the direction of the same mason. The entranceway's stone work has been purposely laid up to restrict entry. The overall design of the structure certainly represents an intent on the part of the builder far beyond that of a simple storage house."

The Upton Chamber, mentioned above by Whittall, is one of the largest and most perfectly built chambers in New England and is all underground. It is, in fact, the reason why Malcolm Pearson got into archaeology in the first place. When he graduated from high school in 1928, his family moved to Upton. *"What do you think of the cave in your backyard?"* the previous owner asked him as his father signed the papers. Malcolm hadn't seen the cave, but he immediately made it a point to seek it out. It was mammoth — a six foot high and fourteen foot long tunnel leading into the side of a hill with an inner chamber of fieldstones, *"like an Eskimo igloo,"* Malcolm thought. The chamber, with a large oval shaped stone weighing several tons as a roof measures twelve feet in diameter and eleven feet high. *"The walls are irregularly shaped stones, fitted together by expert artisans"* says Malcolm. He attempted to trace the cave back in history as far as he could. The town was settled in 1735 and historical records brought the chamber back to that time. *"I wrote to the Smithsonian Institute and sent them information and photos, and they replied stating that 'it might be a vegetable cellar.' It's too damp and there's no ventilation for the preservation of perishables in the chamber. The entrance is too narrow to fit a wheelbarrow through, or even a bushel basket. It just wasn't a food storage chamber. Their reply got me so agitated that I boldly entered the field of archaeology."* When town fathers decided to write the history of Upton in 1935, Malcolm was asked to write about the chamber. *"The cave reposes as mute evidence of a hardy race,"* he wrote, *"who built a lasting memorial to their skill. Time may never reveal its builders, but all will wonder at this masterpiece of stone masonry."*

Byron Dix and Jim Mavor have recently revealed fascinating information concerning the Pearson Chamber at Upton. On nearby Pratt Hill they discovered four cairns and learned that back in history, they were in alignment with the chamber, meaning that the chamber was once an observatory and calendar. By following the direct astronomical alignment of the stars of the cluster Poladies through the ages, on line with the chamber and the cairns at Pratt Hill, Dix and Mavor were able to date the chamber at Upton to 710 A.D.

In Ireland and Scotland most beehive chambers are found along the sea-coast, but in New England many are found on the sloping banks of rivers, brooks, lakes and near swampy ground. In fact, some of the most remarkable chambers are found in the mountains of Vermont. In one chamber in Putney, Vermont, recently excavated by Jim Whittall and a crew from Early Sites, charcoal was found and analyzed at Geochron Laboratory in Cambridge, resulting in a radio-carbon age of 492 A.D., exactly 1,000 years before Columbus made his famous voyage. In central Vermont, at a place called South Royalston, a unique area of ancient architecture has been kept secret for almost nine years by archaeologists who wished to probe its secrets in peace. The site, dubbed Calendar I by Byron Dix and Jim Mavor, holds five chambers, six standing stones and six stone mounds, covering an area of five square kilometers. On the site is also an old Indian fort, and Mavor reports that *"the results of archaeological excavation of five standing stones and three stone chambers at Calendar I suggest that prehis-toric Native Americans played a role in the design and construction of these lith-ic features. "* Yet, the site also shows a strong Irish influence. On the side of a hill which slopes down into a natural bowl called Elephant Valley stands a clus-ter of three upright standing stone slabs, only 600 feet from a chamber and near a large cairn. Two of these slabs contain linear markings thought to be ogam. Barry Fell recognized the markings as vowel-less ogam, dating from the second to the eighth century A.D., but the messages are unintelligible. Beside the ogam are chiseled patches or squares in the rocks, almost looking like windows, and some like windows within windows. Only one other place in the world is known to have a standing stone with similar markings, and that's on the Dingle Peninsula, County Kerry, Ireland, in an ancient graveyard. It has a square divid-ed into four squares, the upper pair of which is again subdivided into four squares, and beside it, in ogam, the inscription *"MARIANA,"* the meaning of which no Irish scholar understands. There are grid markings with linear markings on stones on the Iberian Peninsula, but they don't resemble the Irish or Vermont stones, and no one seems to know what these grid markings mean. Jim Whittall concludes that *"The Kinard East Irish inscription at Dingle dates to somewhere between the 7th and 9th centuries, and it's my strong opinion that the Calendar I stones were incised in a pre-Colonial period, perhaps as early as 500 A.D., and they represent a carefully organized statement of considerable importance. Certainly they deserve more respect and attention to their significance than pass-ing them off as idle doodling by a stone mason or a farm boy. Such close-mind-ed attitudes lead only to the eventuality of the site's destruction, which has hap-*

pened more than once both in Vermont and Ireland."

Whittall, with Judy Foley, also uncovered artifacts of ancient vintage near a four by six foot monolith they were excavating, as well as *"blotches of powdered graphite in front of the slab, away from the base."* In ancient times, graphite was used for body paint, water-proofing and in Pagan ceremonies.

Near the same location, they uncovered a cobblestone walkway that was completely fire burned, and, says Whittall, *"this peculiar pavement aligns perfectly on the Equinox."* Like much of the stonework throughout New England, the purpose of this burned-cobbled walkway remains a mystery.

After some eight years of archaeoastronomical investigations at the Calendar I site in South Royalston, Vermont, Byron Dix and Jim Mavor of Woods Hole Associated Scientists recently revealed thirty-two astronomical alignments to solar events from one single observation point. *"Of these alignments,"* say Mavor and Dix in their *Progress Report on New England Archaeoastronomy,"twelve correlate with major calendrical solar events, two with lunar events, and one north and one south within one degree declination. The remaining sixteen alignments are limited to the declination range ... A clear pattern has emerged in which marked stones are found only in places which ultimately turn out to have astronomical associations ... In New England, stones with slash marks have been found in almost every stone context: ledge, primary stones in stone rows, standing stones, stone mounds and embrasures, in an archaeological context possibly predating 700 years before the present."*

Unfortunately, this priceless ancient observatory in Vermont is being picked apart by local scavengers. One of the large marked standing stones has recently been carted off to decorate a local Yuppie's flower garden. He is probably a Samuel Eliot Morison follower and believes that all chambers are *"Colonial vegetable storage huts,"* and all marked standing stones are the result of *"being gouged by a plow"* or are merely *"frostpits."* As today's so-called *"maverick archaeologists"* are trying to bring the Dark Ages to light, Morison's so-called classic scholars are trying to drag us all back to the Dark Ages, and in the process, some of America's cherished ancient relics are being destroyed. American was, and is, Saint Brendan the Navigator's Promised Land. And today we have some pretty convincing evidence to back up his claim.

Top is a rock cairn measuring about 25 feet by 200 feet at Hopkington, Massachusetts. Below is a cairn similar in height and length located in Heapstown, County Sligo, Ireland, and the bottom right is a cairn 45 feet wide by 120 feet in length, shaped like a boat, in Thompson, Connecticut. No one knows for sure what these cairns represent or who built them, but they are found throughout New England and Ireland and parts of Scandinavia. They may be sacred places of the ancients, as well as burying mounds.

Jim Whittall at the Holy Well of Saint Columbo, Donegal, Ireland, which is sur-rounded by a rock cairn. Jim holds the large diamond-shaped quartz stone at the mouth of the well in his left hand, and the white quartz stone he uncovered at Gungywamp, Groton, Connecticut, is in his right hand. Obviously there is some religious significance to these diamond-shaped white quarts tones, but what it is, archaeologists have yet to discover.

Irish historian Michael Poynder holds a white limestone diamond he retrieved from a Bronze Age stone chamber in Ireland. White quartz and limestone rocks are also prevalent in New England chambers, often shaped into diamonds and triangles.

Triangular "lug stones" standing side by side in an ancient wall at Carvin, Ireland.

White quartz triangle found at chamber site in Moodus, Connecticut.

One of the two chambers at Moodus, Connecticut.

White quartz diamond found at Gungywamp, Connecticut.

Beam of sunlight shines through tube in stone chamber at Gungywamp and illuminates a white stone in a small beehive crypt, and has been doing so for centuries on two days each year, September 21st and March 22nd.

At sunrise in December, facing a standing stone at an ancient Red Paint mound in Salisbury, Massachusetts, this diamond of purple light was produced on the face of the stone. Is this a clue to the ancients' reverence to the diamond symbol?

Double circle of stones at the center of the Gungywamp site at Groton, Connecticut. Thought to be an Indian name, in Gaelic, "Gungywamp" means, "Church of the people."

Archaeology students led by David Barron, president of the Gungywamp Society, dig for artifacts and information about the mysterious site which was discovered by the first white settlers into Connecticut in 1654.

Rean Whittall, Jim's daughter, is pictured here after she accidentally uncovered ancient ogam script carved into a boulder at Gungywamp.

David Barron stands at the opposite end of the 38-foot underground tunnel (left) discovered in 1938 when the entrance was exposed (right) after a large oak tree was uprooted at Montville, Connecticut. This souterrain and chamber are just across a brook from the Gungywamp site.

Malcolm Pearson climbs down into the 60-foot tunnel at the Goshen, Massachusetts chamber, located not far from the Connecticut River.

*(Top) A typical chamber in Ireland dating back to the Bronze Age.
(Bottom) Dick Lynch crouches inside the "Worcester" Airport
Chamber," in Leicester, Massachusetts, just one of over 275 chambers
in New England.*

Myra Pearson stands at the entrance of one of the largest chambers found in New England at Upton, Massachusetts. called the "Pearson Chamber," it was recently discovered that it is also an ancient astronomical observatory.
Photo by Malcolm Pearson.

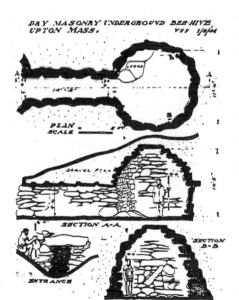

DRY MASONRY UNDERGROUND BEE-HIVE
UPTON MASS.   VFF 1/4/64

LEDGE

PLAN
SCALE

GRAVEL FILL

SECTION A-A

SECTION
B-B

ENTRANCE

Sketch by Vincent Fagan of inside the beehive chamber at Upton and the long drywall tunnel leading into it.

Photo taken inside the Upton chamber in 1900.

Standing stone on Dingle Peninsula, Ireland (left) has strange grid markings carved into it. Such grid markings have been found on stones in the Iberian Peninsula and (right) on standing stones and chamber slabs at South Royalston, Vermont. The other markings on the stone, Barry Fell says, are ancient Celtic ogam.

Elephant Valley in South Royalton, Vermont, known to archaeoastronomers as "Calendar I Site," is where Byron Dix and Jim Mavor made 32 astronomical alignments to solar events from just one observation point. The chambers shown here are where Hannah Hendee and nine children hid out during an Indian raid on October 16, 1780. These chambers and the strange standing stones surrounding them, were here long before Vermont was settled , sometime between 500 and 800 A.D.

Photo courtesy of Margery Greenleaf.

IV
The Great Stone Knight

In Robert Lewis Stevenson's classic, *"Treasure Island,"* the pirates led by Long John Silver, with the boy Jim Hawkins, follow a treasure map to a deserted island, which isn't deserted at all, but is the home of a long lost adventurer named Ben Gunn. Stevenson lived at Edinburgh, capital of Scotland, only a few miles from Rosslyn castle, a medieval structure. The castle is shrouded in mystery, and is the ancestral home of the clan Sinclair, originally St. Clair. Here, it is said, are kept many deep secrets and vast treasures. More than one Sinclair was an elite Templar Knight of the Crusades, attempting to claim the Holy Land for Christianity. Some members of the family were deemed keepers of holy treasures for European royalty and religious leaders. Allied to the Sinclairs were the Gunns, *"a warlike and ferocious family,"* claims *"The Scottish Clans and Their Tartars"* book, that *"emerged as a clan in the 13th century, after Gunn, said to be the son of Olav the Black, Norse king of man and the isles...through marriage to the heiress....of the Earl of Orkney and Caithress..."* A question that I ponder in my mind to this day, which may never be answered is, why did author Robert Lewis Stevenson choose a man named Ben Gunn to be the sole inhabitant of an unknown island in the West that contained a vast buried treasure? Was Stevenson aware of one of the great secrets of Rosslyn Castle, which he chose to reveal in a work of fiction, or was it just a coincidence that he used the name Gunn? The following account is fact, not fiction. After reading it, I'll let you decide if the author of *"Treasure Island"* was really revealing to us a long kept secret from the Sinclair's Rosslyn Castle.

The Sinclairs, like the Gunns, were of Norman stock, descendants of the Vikings. William, son of Comte de Saint Clair of Normandy, entered England with William the Conqueror in 1066, settled in Scotland, and like the Gunns, mixed it up with the Celts to create a breed of their own. As in Ireland, where the saying is *"the Normans became more Irish than the Irish themselves,"* such was the case in Scotland as well.

When the Crusades began in 1096 A.D., soldiers and knights from most European countries answered the call of Catholic Pope Urban II to rid the Holy Land, and specifically Jerusalem, of Muslim Arabs and Turks. Within three years Jerusalem was in Christian hands, and within two weeks of the fall of Jerusalem, Pope Urban died. The Crusader Knights, most of them noblemen of Europe, decided to vote for a King of Jerusalem, to which the Catholic priests objected. However, treasure-seeking warriors, and not holy men, now held sway in the Holy Land. A pious yet fierce Crusader knight from France, Godfrey deBouillon, won the vote and agreed to be leader, or Master, but not King of Jerusalem. His title was *"Defender of the Holy Sepulchre."* He then led the Crusaders off to fight the Egyptian army, which was more than five times their size. The knights slaughtered the Egyptians and obtained so much gold and jewelry that they couldn't carry it all. Many satisfied knights and peasant soldiers returned to Europe with their riches, with but 300 knights and 2,000 Christian soldiers remaining in Jerusalem. Guarding the Holy City with Godfrey deBouillon was his friend and fellow knight from Rosslyn, Scotland, Henry Saint Clair. To protect the many Pilgrims who then flocked out of Europe to visit the Holy Land for the first time, a group of nine knights, including Sinclair and the second leader of Jerusalem, French knight Baudion, organized a brotherhood called *"Templar Knights"* to protect the visitors as they trudged treacherous roads to Jerusalem. Under a papal decree, these nine warrior-monks were independent of all secular authority, and were answerable to the Pope only. Although they had sworn a vow of poverty, these priestly knights became very rich over the years.

Al-Harawi, an Arab historian who visited Jerusalem in the 12th century, wrote that, *"the mosque (Al-Haram Al-Sharif — Dome of the Rock) now became a Christian church which is called 'Templum Domini.' The Crusaders built an altar on the sacred Rock and filled the church with paintings and images...A gold cross placed on the dome, and the image of Jesus, made of gold and studded with diamonds was fastened to the door....In addition to above there was a picture of Solomon, son of David, on the wall facing the door of the cave beneath the Rock, and to the north of the building there were houses of the priests (Templars), built on beautiful pillars...It is customary for Crusaders to break off pieces of the Rock to carry back to Constantinople and Sicily as souvenirs. The priests also sold pieces of the rock to pilgrims who carried them back to Europe as holy relics. These pieces, sold for their weight in gold, brought large revenues to the priests, but the practice was stopped lest the entire Rock be removed in this way. To save it, the Crusader kings covered it with marble and built around it an iron grille."*

Remarkably, having visited the Dome of the Rock, I saw that this iron grille remains as the only testament, except for ruined forts, that the Crusaders were ever in the Holy Land. Their influence, however, is far reaching in almost all countries to this day, and the Dome of the Rock is responsible for much of this influence. This mosque was designed by Arabs, modeled after the Church of the Holy Sepulchre and using its exact measurements. The church is only some twenty blocks away, standing over the supposed tomb of Christ. Today, some Protestant denominations believe the tomb is not located under the pillars of the Holy Sepulchre structure, but in a garden in another part of the city. The Dome of the Rock structure, with its copper and gold rounded roof and beautiful tile facade, courtyards, and fountains, covers one-sixth of the area inside the walls of the Holy City. It is not only the most prominent structure in the city, but the holiest of ancient relics to Jews, Muslims, and Christians alike. It is here that the ancient Jewish temple stood where Christ preached and drove out the money-changers, shouting. It is bordered by the *"Wailing Wall,"* cherished by the Jews and once part of Solomon's Temple, built to God: *"Ninety feet long and forty feet broad, and the height of it was forty-five feet,"* reads the Old Testament. *"The house was built of stone made ready before it was brought there, so that there was no sound of hammer or axe or any tool in the house while it was being built. The walls and floors and ceilings of the house were the boards of cedar, and Solomon covered the floors with planks of fir. And he covered the whole house with pure gold, and the whole altar in the holy of holies was covered with pure gold..... The house was seven years in building....And Solomon brought the things which David his father had dedicated. The silver and gold and the vessels he put among the treasures of the Lord. Then Solomon assembled the elders of Israel and all the heads of the tribes, that they might bring the ark of the Lord's covenant into the temple at Jerusalem....There was nothing in the ark except two tablets of stone which Moses had put there at Horeb when the Lord made a covenant with the children of Israel when they came out of the land of Egypt,"* so reads the Holy Bible. Solomon's Temple was later destroyed by the Chaldeans.

The people of Islam, Muslims-Mohamadins, considered the rocky cliff which the copper-gold dome covers, to be where the prophet Mohammed stepped off into paradise. His footprint is embedded in the rock. The mosque sitting beside the Dome of the Rock is the religious center of the Muslims and considered most holy, with only Mecca in Saudi Arabia being more sacred to them. Even to those without any religious bent, the Dome of the Rock and courtyards surrounding it are an historical hot bed, and an archaeological one as well. Is the Ark of the Covenant still buried, with Solomon's treasure, underground, possibly in the cave under the great rock at the Dome of the Rock? Could the Templar Knights, digging under their homes, *"North of the Dome of the Rock,"* have found some of the holy treasure of Solomon and confiscated it when the Muslim Saladin recaptured Jerusalem from the Crusaders in 1296 A.D.? That was the rumor in Europe at the time. After some 200 years in the Holy Land, the Christian Kingdom of Jerusalem was no more. The Templars retreated with the other Crusaders, many of them descendants, great grandsons of the original crusaders, and set up new headquarters in France. After some twenty years of existence, the Templars allowed an expansion of their order from the original nine knights, many of the new members being blood relatives. Templar Knights remained a secret mysterious group of great wealth and power, guardians of all holy relics and keepers of the treasury. They became bankers and lenders of money to European monarchs, merchants, and religious leaders. They built and captained their own fleets of vessels for trade, exploration and battle, excelling in navigational skills. In France they remained subject to no one but the Pope.

On Friday the thirteenth, in October of 1307, King Philippe of France could stomach the wealth, power, pride, and arrogance of the Templar Knights no longer. The King convinced Pope Clement V that the Templars weren't the pure, obedient knights of the Crusades, but were foul, nasty fornicators, and if he were allowed to interrogate a few of the number, he would prove their disloyalty to God and king. Clement reluctantly agreed to let Philippe prove his point, and the great Inquisition was underway. There were raids by the King's men on all Templar strongholds. The English knights were warned of the coming raids in time for them to escape. Many of the Scots and French knights, although not forewarned, made for the fleet of ships and escaped. Most of the knights, however, were captured, imprisoned and tortured into false confessions of misconduct, or were burned at the stake. The great treasure trove of the Templars, which the King wished most of all to capture, eluded his greedy fingers and was whisked away, to where, no one knows to this day. Many believe it went with the Scots knights to Sinclair Castle at Rosslyn, where they sailed for safe haven to the Firth of Forth. Ironically, it was the Scots Templars who saved the King of Scotland, Robert the Bruce, from the invading English at the Battle of Bannockburn at about that same time. The Templars, led by William Sinclair, had only recently arrived in Rosslyn and were in hiding when they got the news of the English army advancing on the Scottish capital. The Templars were thought to be a *"straggling band of highlanders,"* and were placed with the *"camp followers, grooms and small folk,"* for the battle had already begun when they arrived and it was thought that they'd only get in the way. As Ronald McNair Scott explains it in his book, *Robert the Bruce, King of Scots, "As the battle was at its peak, neither side giving an inch, a signal was given to the watchers on Gillies Hill. And over the crest appeared all the camp followers (including the Templars), servants, and those who had arrived too late for Bruce to incorporate in his formations, rank upon rank in massed array, with broad sheets for banners upon poles and spears. As they came down the hill and saw the battle below them and the English beginning to falter, they gave a great shout of, "Upon them upon them!" When the English saw this vast host approaching, they believed it to be a second Scottish army and all hope left them. Their slow retreat disintegrated into a panic-stricken rout and each man thought only of how to flee."* The Templars had saved the day for Scotland, but they never got, nor wanted, credit for this. They wanted their presence in Scotland to be kept secret.

When King Robert the Bruce died in 1329, his heart was cut from his body and given to his most trusted warriors, James Douglas and Templar Knight William Sinclair of Rosslyn, to be taken by them to Jerusalem to be laid at the Holy Sepulchre. On their way, they stopped in Spain and went into battle with other knights against the Moors. In a fierce battle, Sinclair and Douglas were surrounded by the enemy and slain. The heart of Bruce, chained to the neck of

Douglas, was removed and returned to Scotland with the bodies of the two knights. Four years later, William Sinclair's son William married the daughter of the Earl of Orkney Islands, whose ancestors were kings of Norway. When this second William was killed in battle in 1358, his son Henry Sinclair became the Baron of Rosslyn in Scotland.

The belief in Scotland and elsewhere in Europe is that Rosslyn castle and the nearby chapel, built by William Sinclair in the early 1400s, holds the vast treasure and holy relics brought to Scotland by the refugee Templar Knights from the Holy Land, via France. Rosslyn Chapel is a rebuilding of the Temple of Solomon. It is called *"Grail Chapel,"* and since the Sinclairs and the Saint Clairs before them were keepers of holy relics, it is thought that the Holy Grail, the cup of Christ drank from with his apostles at the Last Supper, is among the treasures, as is *"The Holy Rood,"* a section of the cross upon which Christ was crucified, bedecked with gold, diamonds, and other jewels. The Templars, who had been driven out of France and excommunicated from the Catholic church by the Pope, were not to reveal to anyone where the treasures and relics were hidden. They, in fact, were instrumental in establishing the secret order of Masonry in Scotland, an organization still flourishing today. The keeper of the Grail, so legend has it, must be a knight without sin, and no one seems better fit to this mold than Henry Sinclair, son of William. It seems that all the European kings and queens put their trust in him. Henry was called to Copenhagen from Rosslyn Castle in 1362 to attend the wedding of Haakon VI, King of Norway, to the princess daughter of the King of Denmark. There he became betrothed himself to Florentia, daughter of King Magnus of Sweden. Three years later, King Peter of Cyprus, who dubbed him *"the Holy St. Clair,"* recruited him to lead knights of Templar from Scotland to Venice to sack Alexandria. They took 300 ships and found great success, but in his absence, his betrothed died. When he returned to Scotland, he married Janet Halyburton, daughter of a Scottish lord. The Scandinavians didn't forget him though, and in 1379, the King of Norway and Sweden installed him as the First Earl of Orkney and Lord of the Shetlands, the outer islands off Scotland, long considered the property of the Norse. Some of the islanders were rebelling, so Henry settled himself with a small army at Orkney and began subduing the rebels. With Sinclair was the knight Sir James Gunn, son of Templar Donald Gunn. Then, in 1380, at Fair (or Fer) Island between Orkney and the Shetland Isles, where Sinclair, Gunn, and their men were chasing down a piratical group of islanders, a strange quirk of fate allied the Scottish knights with a crew of Venetians, led by famous navigator Sir Nicolo Zeno. Marco Barbaro wrote of Zeno's adventures 28 years later, and an extensive narrative was published by a descendant of Zeno in 1558, but not translated into English until 1873. In the report, Barbaro calls Sinclair, *"Zicno,"* which Sinclair called himself in Latin, *"Sancto Claro,"* pronounced *"Zinclo."* The *"Zeno Narrative"* uses the name *"Zichmni,"* when referring to the princely chief Sinclair. Excerpts from the narrative are as follows:

"*Nicolo...has a very great desire to see the world and to travel and make himself acquainted with the different customs and languages of mankind. So he had a vessel made and equipped from his own resources, for he was a rich man. And he sailed out of our seas and passed the Strait of Gibraltar, steering always to the north with the object of seeing England and Flanders. Being, however, caught in those seas by a terrible storm, he so tossed about for many days by the seas and the wind that he did not know where he was. When he discovered land at last, as he was not able to beat against the violence of the storm, he was cast on the Island of Frislanda (Fair Island). The crew, however, were saved, and most of the goods that were in the ship. The people of the island came running in great numbers with weapons to attack Sir Nicolo and his men, who were exhausted with their struggles against the storm and...they would doubtless have been very badly treated if a certain chieftain had not fortunately happened to be near the spot with an armed retinue. When he heard that a large vessel had just been wrecked upon the island, he hurried in the direction of the noise and outcries from the attack on our poor sailors. He drove away the natives, addressed our people in Latin and asked them who they were and where they came from. And when he learned that they came from Italy and that they were men of that country, he was exceedingly pleased. Promising them all that they would not be made captive and assuring them that they had come into a place where they would be well treated and very welcome, he took them under his protection and gave his word of honour that they were safe. He was a great lord and possessed certain islands...lying not far from Frislanda. His name was Zichmni. Besides being the lord of these small islands, he was Duke of Soranto (Caithness) which lay over against Scotland.*

...As well as Zichmni being the man I have described, he was warlike and valiant and especially famous in naval exploits....Anxious to win more renown by deeds of arms, he had come with his men to attempt the conquest of Frislanda, which is an island rather larger than Ireland.

This fleet of Zichmni consisted of thirteen vessels. Two only were rowed with oars, the rest were small barks and one was a ship....

So far my account is taken from a letter sent by Sir Nicolo to Sir Antonio Zeno, his brother, asking him to find some vessel to bring him out to him. Since Antonio had as great a desire as his brother to see the world and its various nations, and to make himself a great name, he bought a ship and directed his course that way. After a long voyage full of many dangers, he joined Sir Nicolo in safety and was received by him with great gladness, as his brother not only by blood, but also in courage.

Sir Antonio remained in Frislanda and lived there fourteen years, four years with Sir Nicolo and ten years alone. Here they won such grace and favour with the prince that, to gratify Sir Nicolo, and still more because he knew very well his value, he made him a captain of his Navy..."

As Zichmni was a man of great enterprise and daring, he had determined to make himself a master of the sea. So he proposed to use the services of Sir Antonio by sending him out with a few small vessels to the west, because some of his fishermen had discovered certain very rich and populous islands in that direction. This discovery Sir Antonio relates in a letter to his brother Sir Carlo in detail in the following manner, except we have changed some of the old words and the antiquated style, but we have left the substance entirely as it was.

"Twenty six years ago four fishing boats put out to sea and encountered a heavy storm. They were driven over the sea utterly helpless for many days. When the tempest died at last, they discovered an island called Estotilanda (Nova Scotia) lying to the west over one thousand miles from Frislanda. One of the boats was wrecked, and six men in it were taken by the inhabitants and brought to a fair and populous city, where the king of the place sent for many interpreters. None could be found that understood the language of the fishermen, except one that spoke Latin, who has also been cast by chance on the same island. Speaking for the king he asked them who they were and where they had come from; and when he relayed their answer, the king wanted them to remain in the country. As they could not do otherwise, they obeyed his command and stayed five years on the island and learned the language. One of them in particular visited different parts of the island and reported that is was a very rich country, abundant in all good things. It is a little smaller that Islanda, but more fertile. In the middle of it is a very high mountain, from which rise four rivers which water the whole country.

The tomb of a crusader knight, with his likeness carved into the coffin (left) and the remains of St. Clair castle at Rosslyn, Scotland (right) where many Templar Knights lie buried.

Photos courtesy of Andrew Sinclair.

Church of the Holy Sepulchre, Jerusalem (left) and Dome of the Rock (right). Their measurements and octagonal design were copied to build churches throughout Europe from the 1100s to the 1400s A.D.

1400 A.D.

A petroglyph of a sailing ship and cross (left) are carved into whale back ledge, Clarks' Point in Machias, Maine. The one mast and high poop decks fore and aft depict a vessel design originating from 1350 to 1450 A.D., much like the sketch (right), a ship design that died out after 1450. Could the rock sculptor be one of Sinclair's vessels, with a fishnet hanging from the stern?

The Zeno Map, with Estotiland being Nova Scotia and Droceo probably New England.

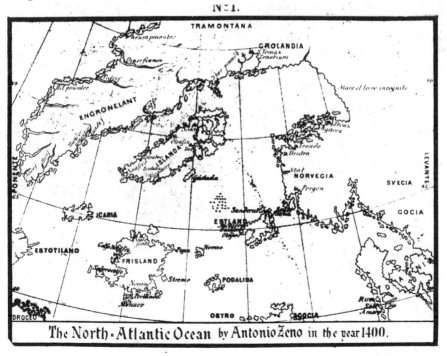

A bronze shield thickly cemented with sea growth is brought up from the shallows off Marshland, Massachusetts by a fisherman in 1954. Note warriors and horses embossed on the shield (lower left). The shield has since disappeared but is thought to have come from a nearby shipwreck where silver spoons have been retrieved by divers, that may well date back to the 1300s.
Photos by Edward Rowe Snow.

Top right) is a similar bronze shield as that found off Marshfield, called the "Achilles Shield," recently sold at a London auction for $677,600. (Bottom) is Medieval armor, including the shield of a Templar Knight of the Crusades on display in Scotland. It also resembles the Marshfield shield.
Photo courtesy of Andrew Sinclair.

The inhabitants are very intelligent people and possess all the arts we do. It is believed that in time past they have had dealings with our people, for he said that he saw in the king's library Latin books, which they do not understand. They have their own language and letters. They have all kinds of metals, but especially they are rich in gold. Their foreign connections are with Engroneland (Greenland), to which they export furs, sulfur and pitch. He says that towards the south there is a great and populous country, very rich in gold (America?). They sow corn and make beer, which is a kind of drink that northern people take as we do wine. They have woods of immense extent. They make their buildings with walls, and there are many towns and villages. They make small boats and sail them, but they have not the lodestone, and they do not know the north by compass bearing.

For this reason these fishermen were highly valued, and the king sent them with twelve boats to the south to a country which they called Drogio (America?). On their voyage they met contrary winds and were in fear for their lives. Although they escaped one cruel death, they fell into another even crueler. For they were taken and most of them eaten by savages, who were cannibals and considered human flesh as very savory meat.

Yet as our fisherman and his remaining companions could show them how to catch fish with nets, their lives were saved. Every day he would go fishing in the sea and in the fresh water and catch a great amount of fish, which he gave to the chiefs. So he grew in favour and he was much liked and held in consideration by everybody.

As this man's fame spread through the surrounding tribes, a neighboring chief became very anxious to have him and see how he practiced his wonderful art of catching fish. Therefore he made war on the chief who had the fisherman, and as he was more powerful and a better warrior, he overcame him in the end. So the fisherman was sent over to him with the rest of his company. During the thirteen years he lived in those parts, he says that he was sent to more than twenty-five chiefs. They were continually fighting among themselves, and only with the purpose of having fishermen to live with them. Forced to wander up and down the country without any fixed home, he became acquainted with almost all that land.

...After having lived so many years in these parts, this fisherman made up his mind, if possible, to return home to his own country. His companions were in despair of ever going home again, but he bade them Godspeed and stayed where they were. He said farewell and made his escape through the woods in the direction of Drogio, where he was welcome and acceptable to its chief, who knew him and was a great enemy of the neighboring chieftain. Again passing through

the hands of the same chiefs, after a long time and with much hardship, he at last reached Drogio, where he spent three years. Here by luck he heard from the natives that some boats had arrived off the coast. Full of hope at being able to make his escape, he went down to the seaside and was delighted to find that they had come from Estotilanda. He asked them to take him with them, which they did very willingly. And as he knew the language of the country, which none of them could speak, they employed him as their interpreter.

Afterwards he traded in their country so well that he became very rich and fitted out a vessel of his own and returned to Frislanda. Then he gave an account of the rich countries he had seen to this nobleman (Sinclair). His sailors had much experience in hearing strange tales and fully believed what they heard. This nobleman is now determined to send me out with a fleet towards those parts. There are so many that want to join in the expedition on account of the novelty and strangeness of the thing, that I think we shall be very well equipped, without any public expense at all."

Such is the tenor of the letter I referred to, which I have set out here in detail in order to throw light upon another voyage which was made by Sir Antonio. He set sail with many vessels and men, but he was not the commander, as he expected to be. For Zichmni went himself. And I have a letter describing that enterprise, which reads:

'Our great preparations for the voyage to Estotilanda began unluckily. For exactly three days before our departure, our fisherman and our guide died. Yet Zichmni would not give up the enterprise, but instead of the deceased fisherman, he took some sailors that had come out with him from the island. Steering west, we discovered some islands subject to Frislanda, and passing by certain shoals, we came to Ledovo, where we stayed seven days to rest and restock the fleet.

After leaving there we arrived on the first of July at the Island of Ilofe (Faroes), and as the wind was fair, we pushed on. Not long after, when we were on the open sea, so great a storm arose that we were continuously working for eight days and driven we knew not where, while many of the boats were lost. At length, when the storm abated, we gathered the scattered boats and sailed with a prosperous wind to discover land to the west. Steering straight for it, we reached a quiet and safe harbour, but there we saw an infinite number of armed people, who came running furiously down to the waterside to defend the island.

Zichmni now caused his men to make signs of peace to them, and they sent ten men to us who could speak ten languages, but we could understand none of them except one that was from Islanda. This interpreter was brought before

- 65 -

*our prince and asked what was the name of the island and what people inhabit-
ed it and who was the governor. He answered that the island was called Icaria,
and that all the kings who reigned there were called Icarim after the first king.*

*...Sailing round the island, he sent all his fleet in full sail into a harbour
which he found on the eastern side. The sailors went on shore to take in wood
and water, which they did as quickly as they could, for fear they might be
attacked by the islanders. And indeed, the inhabitants did make signals to their
neighbors with fire and smoke, and took to their arms with more coming to their
aid. They all came running down to the seaside to attack our men with bows and
arrows, so many were slain and several wounded. Although we made signs of
peace to them it was no use. Their fury increased more and more, as though they
were fighting for their very existence.*

*Forced to depart, we sailed in a great circle round the island, always
followed on the hill tops and along the sea coasts by an infinite number of armed
men. Doubling the north cape of the island, we came upon many shoals, among
which we spent ten days in continual danger of losing our whole fleet; but fortunately the weather kept very fine. All the way until we came to the east cape, we
saw the islanders still on the hill tops and by the sea coast, keeping up with us
and howling and shooting at us from a distance to show their hatred of us. So we
resolved to put into some safe harbour and see if we might once again speak with
the interpreter, but we failed in our objectives. For the people were more like
beasts than men and stood always prepared to beat us back if we should attempt
to come on land.*

*When Zichmni saw that he could do nothing, he realized that the fleet
would fall short of provisions if he were to persevere in his attempt. So he took a
fair wind and sailed six days to the west; but when the wind shifted to the south-
west and the sea became rough, we sailed four days with the wind aft. Then at
last we discovered land. As the sea ran high and we did not know what country
it was, we were afraid at first to approach it. But by God's blessing, the wind
lulled, and then a great calm came on. Some of the crew then pulled ashore and
soon returned with the joyful news that they had found an excellent country and
a still better harbour. So we brought our barks and our boats in to land, and we
entered an excellent harbour, and we saw in the distance a great mountain that
poured out smoke. This gave us hope that we should find some inhabitants in the
island. Although it was a great way off, Zichmni would not rest without sending
a hundred soldiers to explore the country, and bring an account of what sort of
people the inhabitants were.*

*Meanwhile, we took on a store of wood and water and caught a con-
siderable quantity of fish and sea-fowl. We also found such a quantity of bird's*

eggs that our men, who were famished, ate of them until they were stuffed full. While we were at anchor here, the month of June came in, and the air in the island was mild and pleasant beyond description. Yet as we saw nobody, we began to suspect that this pleasant place was uninhabited. We gave the name of Trin to the harbour and the headland which stretched out into the sea we called Capo di Trin (Cape Breton?). After eight days the hundred soldiers returned and told us that they had been through the island and up to the mountain. The smoke naturally came from a great fire in the bottom of the hill, and there was a spring giving out a certain matter like pitch which ran into the sea, and there were great multitudes of people, half-wild and living in caves. These were very small of stature and very timid; for as soon as they saw our people, they fled into their holes. Our men also reported that there was a large river nearby and a very good and safe harbour.

When Zichmni heard this and noticed that the place had a wholesome and pure atmosphere, a fertile soil and good rivers and so many other attractions, he conceived the idea of staying there and founding a city. But his people had passed through a voyage so full of hardship that they began to murmur, saying that they wished to return to their own homes. The winter was not far off, and if they allowed it to set in, they would not be able to get away before the following summer. He therefore kept only the rowboats and those people who were willing to stay with him, and he sent all the rest away in the ships. He appointed me against my will to be their captain. I had no choice, and so I departed and sailed twenty days to the east without sighting any land. Then I turned my course towards the island of Neome (Orkneys). Knowing the country, I saw I was past Islanda, and as the inhabitants were subject to Zichmni, I took in fresh stores and sailed with a fair wind in three days to Frislanda. The people there thought they had lost their prince because of his long absence on the voyage we had made. So they gave us a hearty welcome.'

What happened afterwards I do not know beyond what I gather from a piece of another letter, which maintains that Zichmni settled down in the harbour of his newly discovered island and explored the whole of the country thoroughly. I know this because of the particular details on the sea charts; but the description is lost. The beginning of the letter runs like this:

'Those things you want to know from me about the people and their habits, the animals, and the countries nearby, I have written in a separate book, which, please God, I shall bring with me...I have also written the life and exploits of Zichmni, a prince who deserves immortal memory as much as any man that ever lived for his great bravery and remarkable goodness...But I will say no more of this in this letter. I hope to be with you very shortly and to satisfy your curiosity on other things by word of mouth.'

"All these letters were written by Sir Antonio to his brother Sir Carlo. I am sorry that the book and much else on these subjects have, I don't know how, been destroyed. For I was only a child when they fell into my hands, and as I did not know what they were, I tore them to pieces, as children will do, and ruined them. It is something which I cannot now recall without the greatest sorrow. Nevertheless, in order that such an important memoir should not be lost, I have put it all in order as well as I could in this narrative. More than its predecessors, the present age may derive pleasure from the great discoveries made in those parts where they were least expected. For our age takes a great interest in new narratives and in the discoveries, made in countries unknown before, by the high courage and great energy of our ancestors."

Obviously Sinclair and some of the men remained behind in what is thought to be Nova Scotia in 1398, but there is no record of how he returned to the Orkney Islands, where he was assassinated by the English in 1400. MicMac Indian legend of a white visitor called Glooscap, who came into Nova Scotia and Maine in a stone canoe which he built himself, leads some to believe that Glooscap (sometimes called Moosecap) is Sinclair and the he built a ship to sail into America. Certainly Sinclair brought experienced carpenters, masons, and blacksmiths with him, for his intent was to establish free and holy settlements in this new land, away from the influence of pope and kings. Another Indian legend, retold in oral history among the Algonquin Indians of New England, is that of the *"Bearded Strangers who taught net-fishing,"* as was related by the shipwrecked fishermen in the Zeno Narrative. The Indian legend, passed down from father to son for centuries, was that one day four great canoes were seen coming toward shore. They had white wings like giant eagles. The man had hair on their heads and faces, and since Indians don't grow hair on their faces, these pale skinned men who came ashore were considered evil. The Indians attacked them, and those who lived were prepared to burn at the stake, roasted, and eaten. Only four men from these great canoes were kept alive. In watching the Indians fish, one of the captives made a net of knotted vine and showed how many fish could be caught in it when drawn underwater. This saved the man's life, for now many of the Algonquin Indians wanted to learn this new fishing method, and the fisherman was passed from village to village so that all Indians could learn.

At Machias, Maine, hammered with a crude pecking instrument into the whale back ledge at Clark's Point, is the petroglyph of a sailing ship with one mast, heading towards a cross, which is also engraved in of rock. There seems to be two poles curving out of the stern of the ship, which have been thought to represent oars, but could very well represent a fishing net. A sketch of the boat and cross was made by Machias native H. R. Taylor in 1868, and the rendering on the ledge facing out to sea is as discernible today as it was then. The type of boat depicted is of European vintage of the period 1350 to 1450 A.D. Its particular deign was not known before that date and not popular after that time. Who produced the petroglyph, we'll probably never know, but the time frame fits into the period of Sinclair's visit to these lands in ships of this type. And if the structure hanging from the stern does represent a fishing net, which was a great revelation to the Indians, then the puzzle is solved.

There is, of course, much debate over whether Sinclair and his men did come to America. Until later in this century, there just seemed to be no proof of his being here. In Nova Scotia, where he supposedly started two settlements, Venetian cannons have been found at Louisburg and St. Peter's Harbors. These were Pietriera cannons, a particular type produced in Venice only up until the year 1400 A.D. Therefore, unless some explorer 100 years later brought these outdated relics to Nova Scotia, it was surely Zeno and Sinclair who brought them. It is also interesting to note that it was the Zeno brothers who first placed cannons aboard ships in the 1300s and proved that they could be successfully fired from a pitching deck. The St. Peter's Harbor cannon, found by Indians, was unfortunately destroyed, but the Louisburg cannon is on display at the Louisburg Museum in Nova Scotia.

The only man-made relic that might conceivably have a connection to the Sinclair exploration of New England is a bronze shield brought up from the shallow depths off Marshfield, Massachusetts in 1954 by a local fisherman. It was thickly cemented with sea growth and showed warriors in battle. Deeply embedded in sand ashore near where the shield was found was a large oak rudder. In the seas, scuba divers have since found intricately designed silver spoons, and it is believed that the vessel from which these items came is buried underwater beneath tons of sand. There is no known wreck off this Brant Rock, Marshfield area that could produce such artifacts. Although a French trading vessel went down somewhere in the area in 1616, the silver spoons and bronze shield are strange objects to be aboard a vessel trading with the Indians. However, they fit the Sinclair time period and items that his expedition might have had aboard. The sea bottom off Brant Rock will be probed within the next few years, and I with others have claimed the area through the Massachusetts Board of Underwater Archaeology in order to search and excavate the sunken vessel that supposedly carried the shield and the spoons. I actually searched for this wreck with historian Edward Rowe Snow back in 1955, but undersea detecting equipment is more sophisticated today, and we hope to uncover 14th century artifacts, and prove that Sinclair did explore New England, beating Columbus to our shores by almost 100 years.

Another even more revealing discovery, however, places Sinclair and his men in America in 1398-99. It was Frank Glynn, the Assistant Postmaster of

Clinton, Connecticut, and an avid amateur archaeologist, who made a startling discovery concerning the life-sized image of a knight in armor drilled into a rock ledge at Westfield, Massachusetts. If this outline of a knight in armor was pounded into a ledge by a member of Sinclair's party, the explorers must have sailed or rowed up the Merrimac River to about Wicksuck Island, then down Stoney Brook, or hiked an ancient trail, into what is now Westford. The knight in the rock is about one mile up the hill from the river, which gives a wondrous view of Boston and the ocean.

It was Malcolm Pearson who led Frank Glynn to the effigy of the knight in 1954. The knight had been punched with a sharp tool into the rock in a series of dots. It stands 6 1/2 feet tall, carrying a sword, broken in the middle, which is a symbol of death, and in the other hand, a shield. Glynn made a sketch of it and later a plaster casting. First public record of the carving was made in Westfield in 1878. Glynn sent his sketch to Professor T. C. Lethbridge, noted English archaeologist at the University of Cambridge. Lethbridge realized that this knight was much like those found sculpted on the covers of tombs in medieval Scotland, and that the punch marks were made by an ancient armorer's punch and hammer, tools belonging to all ancient armorers who accompanied knights. What Professor Lethbridge found most intriguing is that the coat-of-arms the Westford knight is holding is probably that of the Gunn family, of Scots-Norse heredity. Could it be then, that Sir James Gunn, Henry Sinclair's trusted friend and lieutenant, is buried beneath the large stone ledge at Westford, possibly having suffered a heart attack while climbing the steep hill in his armor? Which brings us back to Scotsman author Robert Lewis Stevenson and his *"Treasure Island,"* with Ben Gunn guarding a vast treasure. Did Stevenson get the germ for this story from the secretive Sinclairs of Rosslyn Castle who told of burying Sir Gunn in a strange land across the sea? And to speculate even further, could Sinclair and his knights have moved the holy treasures, placed under his safe keeping, from Rosslyn Chapel to this Promised Land to keep it from the pope or the English? If so, where could that treasure be hidden?

British artist Marriana Lines makes a rubbing of the knight at Westford, Massachusetts, using organic material on cloth in 1991.
Photo by Jim Whittall.

Author Bob Cahill stands over the Westford Knight where a stone has recently been erected to tell the Sinclair story.
Photo by Steve Harwood.

Another carving punched out of rock in the same style as the Westford Knight was discovered by the first settlers on an ancient trail at Westford less than a mile from the knight. The one-masted vessel is of the type used in the late 14th century, but the downward pointing arrow and the number "184" has no recognizable significance.

LEGEND- "...obsolete before Columbus discovered America" -found in Louisburg Harbor

The ancient Venetian cannon, thought to be brought to Nova Scotia by Zeno and Sinclair, was found in Louisburg Harbor and is on display at the Louisburg Museum in Nova Scotia.
Photo by Malcolm Pearson.

The Westford Knight, punched into a large rock slab with armorer's tools, was made into a plaster cast by Frank Glynn, producing this sketch. Note that the coat-of-arms on the shield he holds is of the Gunn family, as depicted in the arms displayed (top right). (Top left) is the emblem of the Knights Templar. A hawk or falcon, seemingly spitting, sits above his sword, and in his right hand seems to be a rose and either rosary beads or a dagger. The great surcoat is typical of outerwear for knights in armor. The cut sword means that this knight died, probably right on the spot there at Westford, and he may be buried at the foot of the large ledge where his image is punched into the rock. Historian Samuel Eliot Morison said that "frost heaves" caused this knight to be outlined on the rock ledge.

V
The Holy Fort

When a skeleton in armor was uncovered from deep in the ground at Fall River, Massachusetts in 1831, the word spread like wildfire, and speculation was intense. Being so close to Dighton Rock, the remains were thought to be those of Leif Ericson's younger brother Thorvald who was killed by an Indian arrow in the armpit during an exploratory voyage from Greenland in the year 1003 A.D. The incident is recorded in the ancient *"Flatey Book"* of Iceland. Thorvald asked his Viking crew to *"bury me in this pleasant place,"* before he died, and they followed his wishes. The *"Flatey Book"* remarks that *"from this headland where Thorvald was buried, the crew could see the Skraeling (Indian) village inside the harbor."* Many believed that Fall River was that harbor. Others had deciphered Norse rune-markings from the carvings at Dighton Rock, and finding the skeleton in armor only added a fitting piece to the puzzle. The description of what was found at the time is as follows:

"Exhumed at Fall River is the skeleton of a man whose breast is protected by an oval plate of brass, and a belt made of hollow tubes of brass and fitted together like a bandolier of ammunition for a firearm. Near the skeleton were found arrowheads made of brass. He was buried in a sitting position, had copper orna-ments and wore chains and collars."

Most people at first could not even consider that this man bedecked in brass could be an Indian, for no one imagined Native Americans wearing such armor and ornaments, but they did. Bartholomew Gosnold and a crew of 32 Englishmen lived at Cuttyhunk Island for over four months in 1602, visiting the Fall River Indians, who he described as *"wearing copper breastplates, smoking pipes steeled with copper, and taking a great store in copper."* One of many not to be swayed in their opinion at the time was Henry Wadsworth Longfellow. *"I consider the tradition sufficiently established,"* he said and he wrote the poem, *"Skeleton in Armor."*

In the poem, the hero of the tale slays an enemy, the father of his lover, and he captures her and takes her for safe keeping to the Newport Tower in Rhode Island, not too far by water from Fall River and Dighton Rock.

> *"There for my lady's dower*
> *Built I the lofty tower*
> *Which, to this very hour,*
> *Stands looking seaward..."*

Now, the maiden has a child by, guess who? She then gets sick and

> *"Death closed her mild blue eyes,*
> *Under that tower she lies;*
> *Ne'er shall the sun arise*
> *On such another."*

Grief stricken, the Viking puts on his full set of brass armor, which is in keeping with what Greenlanders wore, and then he falls upon his own spear, committing suicide, thus becoming the skeleton in armor at Fall River. The popular poem, of course, made the assumption popular that the skeleton was indeed a Viking from Greenland.

In 1921, five more skeletons were unearthed from a cellar hole in Charlestown, Rhode Island, not far by the sea from what is know as Newport's *"Viking Tower."* They, too, created a controversy that is still simmering. Three of the skeletons were missing skulls, but that wasn't as intriguing as was the large rusted cannon and sword found entombed with them. The cannon was an ancient breech-loader, but the breech was missing, and the sword was Spanish, dating to the late 1400s. Jim Whittall, in an attempt to date the cannon, sent information and photos to museums and historical societies in Europe, one being *"Directo do Servico Historic Militar"* in Lisbon, Portugal. The reply from Jose Varela Rubim, Tenente-Coronel, was: *"We think that the cannon was made in Portugal. We have a similar one here at the Military Museum, although this one is larger. This type of ordnance possibly originated in Italy in the beginning of the 15th century, was named there 'Petarar" as it threw a stone ball....This type of ord-nance was made in Portugal, but the gun in question is of the early type, and of the 15th century. In Portugal this gun was named as cao (dog) and the type as Falca (stone-thrower Falcon)."*

The cannon and sword are now under the care and custody of the Rhode Island Historical Society at the John Brown House in Providence, and the mortal remains of the first skeleton are at Brown University. Whittall concluded, *"Charlestown, Rhode Island, is not too far by boat from the inscribed Dighton Rock, located on the tidal Taunton River which flows to the sea nearby. There is a strong case for some of the markings on the rock having been placed there by Miguel Cortereal from Portugal in 1511. Could this cannon possibly be from his ship?"* Which brings up a further question — could one of these skeletons possibly be him or his brother? There are many unanswered questions concerning this tomb of five: Why were three missing their heads? Were they victims of a battle? Were they white men or Native Americans, or some of each nationality? We'll probably never know. The only thing we do know is that the Cortereal brothers and their crews were lost somewhere off our coast within a year or so of each other, and no trace of them or their vessels has ever been found. That is, not until a Portuguese cannon and Spanish sword dating back to the early 1500s were uncovered at Charlestown, Rhode Island.

And what of these elusive Greenland Vikings or Norsemen? Is there any substantial evidence at all that they came here to New England? The answer is a definitive *"Yes,"* but like the two dramatic skeleton finds, much of what appears to be Norse is not, and some of what appears to be American Indian, is actually Norse, or at least, may be Norse. Our old nemesis Samuel Eliot Morison, of course, believes nothing here in New England is Norse, yet he has satisfied himself that Leif Ericson settled just north of here in 1000 A.D. when he was 18 years old.

Leif Ericson, son of Eric the Red, founder of Greenland, went on his first trans-Atlantic voyage as navigator at age 17 in an 80-foot sailing *"Knorr."* As Iceland's *"Floamanna Saga,"* written some 100 years later reads, *"In the year 999 A.D., Leif sailed to Norway with goods from Greenland to trade, without stopping at Iceland on the way there."* This is an 1,800 mile long non-stop voyage by a teenager, and the first mention of Leif Ericson in any of the sagas. He remained in Norway for the winter, was converted from Paganism to Catholicism, and returned home to Greenland in the spring. In spreading the word of Christ throughout the colony to some 2,000 Icelanders who now lived in Greenland, he visited the home of fisherman and trader Bjane Herjulfson. The fisherman said he and his crew had been blown off course coming to settle in Greenland and had found fertile lands with great tall trees south of Greenland. The Vikings needed timber for roofs, to make ships, and for fire wood. They depended on driftwood and inferior trees from Labrador for building. Leif, with 36 fellow Greenlanders, left their homeland that summer and ventured south. Their landfalls and their activities are well documented in three ancient Norse sagas, but exactly where they landed is disputed till this day. Leif's first landfall was a place they called *"Helluland,"* meaning *"land of rocks."* Some historians believe this was Labrador, but the Greenlanders already had a name for Labrador, where they ventured often. They called it *"Furdustrand,"* meaning *"land of frost."* That means that *"Helluland"* may be the northern tip of Newfoundland, separated from Labrador by only a few miles of water at the Strait of Belle Isle.

It is here at this northern tip of Newfoundland that Norwegian archaeologist Helge Ingstad uncovered and excavated a great Norse house with hard clay floor and a fire pit in the center in 1960. Radio-carbon dating reveals that a fire burned in the house in 1000 A.D. or shortly thereafter. The ruins of other smaller houses, plus a few small artifacts, have been found nearby; a soapstone, a spindle-whorl, and a bronze coat pin. These ruins at L'Anse Aux Meadows,

Newfoundland, are obviously Norse, built by the Greenland colonists, and a wonderful discovery, but Samuel Eliot Morison concluded that this was the *"Great Vinland"* discovered by Leif Ericson, when obviously it isn't. Morison states, *"It seems beyond reasonable doubt proved this place to have indeed been Vinland....So, now that the location of Vinland has been solved, we may proceed with the story as told in the sagas."* Let us indeed proceed, for the sagas tell us that Leif and his crew continued south and sailed to *"Markland,"* meaning *"woodland."* Some historians believe that Markland is Newfoundland and others that it is Nova Scotia. Whichever, the Vikings had to leave this land quickly, for a Nor'easter was in the sky, and it's always best to ride out these three day storms away from land. *"After two to five days of sailing in a southwesterly direction, they sighted land again."* At this third landfall, the crew described it as *"beautiful land with wonderful white sand...We first landed·at an island and sipped sweet dew from the grass."* Then they *"sailed through a sound that lay between the island and that cape, which projected northward from the land itself."* They were sailing westward now *"at a peninsula's sharp elbow,"* where they encountered *"extensive shoals."* This just sounds too much like Martha's Vineyard and the tip of Cape Cod and Chatham, but of course, we can't be sure. This was the place Leif and his men built a large house, the sagas tell us, and spent a very mild winter. The only place you might find a mild winter in New England is at Cape Cod, or possibly the Newport, Rhode Island area. Leif said that they *"found vines and grapes."* The German *"Tyrker,"* who was with them, commented, *"I was born in the south where neither vines nor grapes are scarce. Leif said we shall have two tasks then, each day we will either gather grapes and cut vines, or fell timber to make cargo for my ship."* Tyrker was excited for now he could make wine, which previously the Vikings of Greenland had to import at expensive prices. Wild grapes, which grow profusely at Cape Cod, were a wonder to the Pilgrims and Puritans as well when they settled in the 1600s. These wild grapes do not grow in mid or upper Maine, Nova Scotia, or Newfoundland, but only from southern Maine through Connecticut. So then, how could L'Anse Aux Meadows, Newfoundland be Vinland, and, pray tell, when did they have a mild winter? Sam Morison explains away the grapes by saying that maybe Tyrker meant *"the wild red currant, the gooseberry, or the mountain cranberry."* This is a very weak argument. Ask some German who *"was born where neither vines nor grapes were scarce,"* if he doesn't really mean *"currants, gooseberries, and cranberries,"* and I think you'll get the raspberry, Sam.

Then Morison writes that Leif *"put the 'Vin' in Vinland, and with such success as to throw off all Vinland seekers for centuries!"* You mean Leif Ericson tried to fool us by calling Vinland the place where he didn't find grapes? Give us a break, Sam. Who was he trying to fool, and why? Says Morison about books on Vinland and Vikings being here in America, *"There are scores of books and articles by associated oddballs."* His books and articles are not, of course, written by an oddball. I'm sorry, Sam Morison followers. I know that there's a statue of him sitting on a rock at the park on Commonwealth Avenue in Boston, and his name is even in Webster's Dictionary, but I don't think he could see the forest for the trees on this one, and I think because he was considered an expert, his arrogance and shortsightedness has caused a crucial setback to history and especially to archaeology in America.

A long house, very much like that uncovered at L'Anse Aux Meadows, Newfoundland, has recently been located in the Buzzard's Bay area on the south coast of Massachusetts near Cape Cod. With stone walls and clay floor, it measures 54 feet by 17 feet, with a dividing wall of stone at the back end and a hearth. It is presently on private property, covered with weeds and brush, only a short distance away from a saltwater estuary. The site parallels foundation remains found at village sites in Greenland. Further north up the Atlantic coast at Cutler, Maine, the remains of what is thought to be the foundations of Viking buildings and a dam were discovered at Norse Pond, but archaeologists have yet to dig at the site, as is the case at Buzzard's Bay. It's interesting to note that no one at Cutler seems to know the real reason the pond where the ruins were found is called *"Norse Pond."*

At Spirit Pond, just west of the Kennebec River in Maine, in the autumn of 1971, Indian artifacts hunter Walter Elliott of Quincy, Massachusetts, stumbled upon four stones with unusual markings. Not understanding what the hieroglyphs on them meant, he brought the fist-sized stones to the Peabody Museum at Harvard College. The experts of Harvard could see that the stones had rune markings and drawings deeply etched into them. One read *"Vin 1010,"* and another read *"Hoob,"* possibly signifying that this was the village *"Hop,"* settled by Viking colonists from Greenland under Thorfinn Karlsefni, who voyaged south some ten years after Leif's journey of discovery. A third eight-inch stone read in runes, *"Henricus in October, 1123 A.D., He sailed sixty-eight days, south thirty-four days, and back thirty-four days."* Bishop Henricus, so history tells us, journeyed to Vinland from Norway via Greenland about the date indicated on the Spirit Pond stone. Another stone had the word *"Miltiaki"* carved into it, which in the old Norse language means, *"As seen by me."* So, could these runestones have been left behind by Bishop Henricus? Also deeply sketched into that stone was a fish, a bird, a deer, a snake, an Indian face, a stick-Indian figure rowing a canoe, a bow and arrow, and a drying animal skin, and below all of this a signature, *"The Rune Monk."* One the back side of one of the carved stones was a crude map of the Spirit Pond area, with an arrow pointing down what is now the Norse River and under the arrow is the name *"Vinland."* If one followed the arrow on the rock, he would sail down the river into the sea and after a few hours, still following the arrow, hit Cape Cod. To say that they caused bedlam in the archaeological world would be an understatement. Although many have accepted the Spirit Pond stones as legitimate Norse artifacts, there are others who believe Walter Elliott made them up himself. Elliott was so furious at the accusations that he reburied his stones at Spirit Pond and refused to tell anyone where they were until the state of Maine reimbursed him for his expenses, which the state did, and then Elliott dug up the stones and turned them over to the state archaeologist.

At Sebec Lake, near Greeley's Landing in Maine, a small runestone was uncovered that reads *"Auth Rekr,"* which Olaf Stranwald interpreted as meaning, *"You'll find good luck if you drift further."* A strange Norse message, but a true one, for *"drifting further"* you come into a fruitful area near Penobscot, still noted for its superior hunting and fishing. At Ellsworth, Maine, at a burial mound uncovered in 1897 and thought to be Indian, was found a runestone which read, *"Sthanar Raith,"* thought to mean *"Here, a fellow named Steinar did rule."* Steinar is an old Norse family name. At nearby Bar Harbor, Maine, a Norse penny dating back to 1068 A.D. was uncovered during an Indian shell heap excavation in 1957. The coin depicts a rooster's head on one side and a Norse cross within a circle on the other. It has been deemed authentic by experts at the National Museum of Norway. Across some sixty miles of sea from Bar Harbor, is Yarmouth, Nova Scotia where they keep their runestone on display, which is said to read, *"Leivur Eriku-Resr,"* meaning *"Leif to Eric, raises this monument."* Also at nearby Tor Bay, Nova Scotia, a Norse battle axe was found by a woman in the fields in 1889. On it is the inscription in old Norse, *"for divine protection."* A similar battle axe with mystic symbols was found under the earth at Rocky Nook in Plymouth, Massachusetts.

There are many runestones that have been uncovered along the New England coast, one of the most popular being a marker in the earth at Hampton, New Hampshire. Locals state unequivocally that it is the grave marker of Thorvald, Leif's younger brother, who followed him almost immediately upon his return to Greenland into Vinland, where he was attacked and killed by Indians. It was near here at Hampton Falls that another stone discussed earlier, found by Francis Healey in 1938, was thought by Professor Olaf Stranwald to be a runic stone. A little further south, at the mouth of the Merrimac River, as well as up the river, Norse artifacts and runes have been uncovered. Seven large boulders with markings on them thought to be runic were discovered along the banks of the river at Newbury and Byfield in the early 1900s. At Salisbury, near the mouth of the river, where Jim Whittall has been leading an archaeological dig for over twenty years, he has uncovered pieces of Indian ware from the 1000 to 1300 A.D. period, which is similar to Norse ware. *"It is of an ancient Swedish design which parallels Norse ware,"* says Whittall. *"We also found a piece of pottery at this ancient Indian site with the carving of a shield with a cross inside it."* Up the river at Bradford, Massachusetts in the 1800s, a crudely chiseled statue was found of a Viking carved into a rock on the river front. It prompted John Greenleaf Whittier, a product of the Merrimac Valley to write his poem, *"The Norsemen."*

All the way up and down the river are mooring holes in the river bank rocks for tying up large ships, which author and historian Frederick Pohl concluded were left by Viking explorers. Even Samuel Eliot Morison had to agree that *"It is true Scandinavians then, as now, liked to moor fore and aft, both to an anchor and to the ring-bolt or tree ashore. But in New England there were plenty of stout trees near shore, and no need to drill holes in the granite rocks."* Similar *"mooring holes"* are found at Bar Harbor and one has to assume that Sam Morison never traveled the Merrimac River, or anchored off the Isles of Shoals, or tried to find a stout tree at places like Land's End, Maine, or many of the other barren Maine islands like Boon Island. There just aren't any stout trees, Sam, and there never were. For example, English explorer John Smith talks about one sick cedar at the Isles of Shoals — so sick that you couldn't tie a ship to it. As Frederick Pohl contends, these crudely made mooring holes, obviously drilled through enormous boulders for the purpose of mooring large vessels, could well have been made to anchor Norse vessels. If not, who made them, when and why? These mooring holes were here when the first settlers came. Other Norse items found here when the white settlers came in 1620 were distinctive wide-eyed Norse cats living with the Indians. They are otherwise only found in Scandinavia, Iceland, and Greenland. The Indians, especially the MicMacs, also played Viking games like lacrosse and practiced Viking funerals. There are also many Norse words in their vocabulary.

At Martha's Vineyard, a six-foot tall rock at Oaks Bluffs overlooking the sea, was said to have a runic inscription on it, visible to sailors plying Nantucket Sound. The rock, however, tumbled from its perch and landed on the beach, face up, and by the early 1900s, storms and sand erosion placed it permanently underwater. A similar seaward facing boulder was discovered on the deserted No Man's Land, a tiny island three miles south of Martha's Vineyard in 1926. The runes on the boulder were said to read, *"Leif Ericson's Island — Thirty Men."* Says Morison, *"It was carved in the twentieth century by some joker,"* and he may be right, for most scholars consider it to have been a hoax. But at any rate, the rock with its markings, joke or not, disappeared underwater in the 1938 hurricane. In Narragansett Bay a large rock with highly eroded runic inscriptions was finally deciphered in 1993 by Dr. Richard Neilsen. It reads: *"Victory of four men at this river."* What victory it means, no one knows. Probably the most dramatic Norse artifact was recently discovered near Dighton Rock. It was a six-inch by nine-inch stone mask bowl. It had been dredged up from the river with sludge and unknowingly dumped into the nearby marsh in the 1970s. A bass fisherman spotted it in the discarded river-bottom sludge and retrieved it. It is made of sandstone, its bowl still saturated with oil. It is thought to be a whale blubber lamp. It has an Eskimo-like face of a tattooed Labrador woman, with a Norse rune carved into the forehead. How did it get into the river, and how long had it been there? We may never know. The mask is now being kept in a safe deposit vault by the finder.

All this Norse activity neat Dighton Rock must bring us back to Carl Christian Rafn, the Danish archaeologist and Director of the National Museum in Denmark, who pronounced in 1837 that, *"some of the markings at Dighton Rock are definitely Norse."* One message on the rock read, he said, *"Thorfinn and his 151 companions took possession of this island,"* and Carl Rafn, a most respected archaeologist, also found the date, *"1131,"* which was about the time Bishop Henricus was supposedly visiting Vinland, so Vatican records in Rome reveal. Henricus also supposedly has close connection with the Newport Tower, as does Carl Rafn. Says Samuel Morison, *"Thomas Webb, secretary of the Rhode Island Historical Society and a corespondent of Carl Rafn...picked on a stone tower at Newport, Rhode Island, to be a surviving Norse structure and Rafn fell for it as such."* Carl Rafn didn't *"fall for it."* He, like Webb, was convinced that the tower was built by the Norse. Eighteenth century historian Samuel Adams Drake called the Newport Tower *"A picturesque ruin, which Danish sauans at once claimed as a work of their countrymen centuries before the arrival of the English."* Today it is called by historians and archaeologists, *"The most controversial building in America."* It is an *"old Viking round tower"* to some and *"an old stone mill"* to others. The latter group believe that this 30-foot, eight-columned, roofless fieldstone structure was built by Governor Benedict Arnold, great grandfather to the Revolutionary War traitor general, in the mid 1600s as a windmill. Carl Christian Rafn announced publicly in 1837 that the *"Newport structure was built in the 12th century by Eric, Bishop of Gardar of Greenland as a church."* To the scholars, the features of the tower did look uniquely Swedish or Norwegian, but the windmill theory seemed to hold sway. There were, however, indisputable facts that seem to rule out its use as a windmill: there's a fireplace on the second floor of the tower, and any fire in a flour mill would have blown up the building long ago. One just does not have a fireplace in a flour mill. Also, there were not only no other stone windmills in New England, but there were never any in the world. Yet, there were once many wooden windmills located near the tower. Why would Governor Arnold go to all the trouble of building one of stone, and then not build it perfectly round? Most windmill experts today don't think the mill, if it was one, could have efficiently crushed anything because the rotating part of the mill would have been lopsided. Also, an excavation of the ground directly under the mill in 1948 uncovered an old clay pipe and a few pieces of broken pottery, but not one remnant of grain. It the tower was a mill there should have been organic grain material in the ground beneath the structure.

"The Newport Tower was found by incontrovertible evidence to have been erected as a windmill around 1675 by a colonial governor of Rhode Island," writes Samuel Eliot Morison. Unfortunately for Sam, the evidence is very weak and certainly not *"incontrovertible"* — you be the judge:

Governor Arnold's will of 1677 mentions "my stone built windmill." If he had written, *"the stone windmill I built,"* the controversy would be over, or if he said, "the *stone built windmill that was here when I bought the land,"* speculation would have been enhanced. When Peter Easton built the first windmill in Newport, it was recorded in town records, as were other windmills as they were erected. Why wasn't Arnold's stone built windmill recorded? Could it be that he converted an old stone ruin into a windmill, which obviously couldn't have worked very well? Could the stone tower have been built as a watchtower and converted into a mill? Newport was founded in 1639, and there is no record of such a watchtower being built. In fact, the first governor, William Coddington is said to have asked the local Indians *"who built this tower?"* There answer was that it was here when their ancestors came to this land. Famous Rhode Island founder and leader of the Baptist religion, Roger Williams, believed that the *"white skinned"* local Indians were of *"Icelandic origin."* Seven years before the settlement of Newport, Sir Edmund Plowden partitioned the Crown to settle Europeans on lands near Newport. In his document, he mentions that, *"thirty idle men as soldiers or gentlemen can be resident in a round stone tower and by turns to trade with the savages and keep their ordnance and arms neat."* Therefore, the tower was apparently there in 1632. William Woods, an Englishman who visited New England from 1629 to 1634, returned home and developed a woodcut map, in which he accurately displays all the new settlements and villages, including Plymouth and Salem as being first (1620 and 1627 respectively). However, he names Plymouth as *"New Plymouth"* on his map and at the location where the Newport Tower stands, he wrote *"Old Plymouth."* Why? We don't know. Did he know or did he hear that there was a settlement at Newport prior to the landing of the Pilgrims at Plymouth, Massachusetts? Or maybe he ventured to that area and saw the tower. There is just little doubt that the tower was there before Benedict Arnold bought the land it stood on in the 1650s.

One important questions asked by scholars is that, if the tower was built by the Norse in the 12th, 13th or 14th century, why didn't explorer Giovanni de Verranzano mention in it in his travels up the coast from Florida in 1524? He stopped at or near Newport naming it, *"Refugio,"* and he and his French crew *"spent many days with the natives, who were friendly and generous, beautiful and civilized."* He further described the local Indians as *"of bronze color, some inclining more to whiteness and others of tawny color."* Other Indians he met traveling further North were *"dark and less civilized,"* allowing some scholars to speculate, like Roger Williams, that the Indians living around Newport had inbred with the Norsemen of Greenland. One reason that Williams had come to his conclusion because the Narragansett Indian language contained Norse words. Verranzano also noted that *"they excel us in size,"* and the Norse were always noted to be giants of men compared to other Europeans. A map published in 1524, based on Verranzano's discoveries for the King of France, has written as a name at the Newport location, *"Norman Villa."* The Newport Tower does indeed resemble villas found in Normandy on the coast of France, built by the Norse. If Verranzano didn't see the Newport Tower, then why is the area called *"Norman Villa"* on his map in 1542?

When Malcolm Pearson escorted Scandinavian scholars and runic experts Magnus Bjorndal and Peter Lovfald to the Newport Tower in 1946, they discovered five rune-type markings cut into the stones of the tower, but they have undergone many interpretations since. Bjorndal believed one of the runes read: *"Hnkrs,"* thought to be the abbreviation of *"Henricus."* If Henricus built the tower, then it was erected in the 12th century, but maybe he was just visiting fellow Norsemen and left his mark on a structure that might have been built 100 years or more before.

Probably the most convincing argument that the tower was not built by Englishmen in colonial times is that the measurements used to build the tower are not English, but are Norse-Germanic linear measurements, also known to Icelanders as the *"fet"* and to Scotsmen as *"the Scottish El,"* which is equal to the English 37.5 inches.

The Journal of the American Society of Engineers in 1960, featured an article by engineer Edward Adams Richardson, who, after long study, had concluded that the Newport Tower was not built as a watchtower, for there are no windows on the north side, and that the arrangements of the other windows date the structure to before the 14th century, and that a fire in the fireplace would send a light out into Narragansett Bay as a signal. Richardson concluded that it was a church and a signaling station. Scholars and technicians of various pursuits have concluded the Newport Tower is everything from a lighthouse to a church to a fort. Fireplace experts claim the flues of the tower's fireplace date to the late 1300s, and could not have been built prior to that time. Says Dr. Johannes Brondsted, Director of the National Museum in Denmark, *"These Medievalisms are so conspicuous that, if the tower were in Europe, dating it to the Middle Ages would probably meet with no protest,"* but here in America, Columbus gets in the way, and the followers of Samuel Eliot Morison won't allow evidence in to dispute Columbus as being the first to America. Writer historian Charles Michael Boland says, *"The only other reason for grown men, including scientists and historians, to pronounce such a structure colonial is stupidity."*

Recently a new ground swell of secret intrigue in enveloping the Newport Tower. There is talk now that it wasn't the Norse of Greenland or Iceland who constructed it, but the Scots-Norse of the Orkneys and Rosslyn, Scotland. The likes of Nivan and Andrew Sinclair, Scotsmen and descendants of *"The Holy Knight,"* Henry Sinclair, have been studying the tower, with archaeological sleuth James Whittall. Could it have anything to, we wonder, with the poem by the great Sir Walter Scott, who wrote,

"From the inner edge of the outer door,
At thirty feet of old Scotch measure,
The passage there, that made secure,
Leads to the holy Rosslyn treasure."

Father Richard Hay, the Sinclair genealogist in the 1800s, wrote that *"before Rosslyn Castle burned and much was destroyed by the fire, it had many secrets to tell."* One secret has just become apparent: the Newport Tower is a duplicate Dome of the Rock and Church of the Holy Sepulchre. To add to the intrigue, when it was suggested by some of the wealthy residents of Newport to sell the land the tower stands on to developers in the mid-1800s, Jewish philanthropist Judah Touro bought the land with the tower on it and deeded it to the city. the park where the tower stands is called Touro Park today and just across the street is the Red Cross building, the red cross being the symbol of the Templar Knights — all just a coincidence, don't you think?

At Rosslyn Chapel, carved in stone are ears of New England corn, shucked, exposing kernels, there is also alloid cacti, used even today in medicine also depicted in stone and also a strictly American commodity. How could a structure built in 1437 Scotland depict items found only in America, unless someone had visited across the Atlantic to see them? Rosslyn Chapel, of course, supposedly contains many hidden and holy treasures and relics. Andrew Sinclair in his 1991 book, *"The Sword and the Grail,"* details how he has used the latest radar devices in an attempt to seek out the treasure, thought to be buried deep beneath the chapel floor in giant vaults. *"The problem is how to reach these vaults,"* says Sinclair. Also buried in these vaults are the Templar Knights in their full armor. Andrew did find a secret chamber in the chapel. *"It was small and arched with stone and I squirmed in, but access to the main vaults beyond has been sealed by a thick wall of stone masonry, and the soggy wood from three coffins had been stacked in front of the blocking wall."* Andrew Sinclair then attempted to drill through the center of the chapel to the roof of one of the vaults, but found it was three feet of solid stone and the drill bit broke. Sinclair concluded, *"The vaults of the Chapel of the Grail would keep their secret shrine. The Saint Clair knights would not be distributed in their tombs."*

Jim Whittall, as new evidence is uncovered, is becoming more and more convinced that the Newport Tower may well have been constructed by Henry Sinclair and his men back in 1398-99. Even some gypsum that was found in the mortar used to bind the stones of the tower probably came from Nova Scotia, where Sinclair built his first settlement, for it is the closest place to New England where gypsum can be found in any quantity. *"I'm convinced it's a church and a fort and an observatory,"* says Whittall.

An aerial photo of the tower was taken in 1939 showing some lines extending under the earth from the northern edge of the tower for about 40 feet. William Godfrey was allowed by city fathers to excavate under the tower in the late 1940s, but he was not allowed to dig the perimeter. Another aerial photo was taken in 1951, which again showed a rectangular area extending about forty feet north underground from the tower. These were shown on the photo as two dark lines with a darker strip, but requests to dig there were refused by the city council of Newport and the Newport Historical Society, who consider themselves guardians of the tower. In 1992, a radar sub-surface profile was made by geophysicist Vincent Murphy, the results of which indicated that there were many *"anomalies"* and *"disturbances under the ground,"* and as Murphy told Whittall, *"more intensified radar surveys are needed."* What, if anything, could be hidden underground beyond the eight pillared ruin of Newport — could it be the holy treasures of Jerusalem, brought here to The Promised Land by warrior knights of the Holy Grail, the keepers of God's treasures? *"How far fetched,"* Sam Morison would say, but he said that about the tower being anything but colonial, and I don't have any doubt that he was wrong about that. Probably Jim Whittall would think that it was preposterous to even contemplate that the Holy Grail and other great treasures might be hidden under the Newport Tower. But if they aren't at Rosslyn Castle, where are they? More research and digging is needed, and as Robert Lewis Stevenson wrote in *"Treasure Island"..."Put your trust in Ben Gunn."*

Two of the Spirit Pond stones, found near the Kennebec River, Maine, by Indian artifact hunter Walter Elliott in 1971, are filled with Norse runes. Note the stone with the hole. It was probably a pendant and reads, "Vinland 1010." These stones are extremely controversial, but have been deemed authentic by many experts.

Photos by Malcolm Pearson.

The ruins of Norse homesteads in Greenland were excavated by archaelogists in 1939, and found in the livingroom of one home was a lump of anthracite coal. The only place in North America where anthracite coal can be found is Rhode Island. Just another bit of evidence that the Greenland Vikings were in New England.

Photo of the ruins of Greenland home, courtesy of Early Sites Research Society.

Five skeletons, a Spanish sword, and a Portuguese rock-throwing cannon of the 1400s, were uncovered in 1921 while digging a cellar hole in Charlestown, Rhode Island. Could this skull shown above be that of Miguel Cortereal the explorer, or his brother?

One of two Viking axes found in Nova Scotia and in Plymouth, Massachusetts. Note the mystical Norse markings near the blade to give the owner good luck.
Photo by Malcolm Pearson.

A large boulder overlooking Narragansett Bay contains a highly eroded Norse rune inscription deciphered in 1993 to read, "Four victorious near the river."
Photo courtesy Early Sites Research Society.

Academic archaeologists have deemed this blubber oil lamp as being the mask of "a tattooed Labrador woman," with a Norse rune embedded in her forehead. It was dredged out of the Taunton River near Dighton Rock.

Photos courtesy of Malcolm Pearson and the Early Sites Research Society.

The Newport Tower

A painting of Newport, Rhode Island in 1735 shows windmills (W) located at the top of the hill, and the tower (T) as a ruin, but Governor Benedict Arnold described the tower as "my stone built windmill," which has caused much dispute over when the tower was built and for what purpose.

Photo courtesy of Early Research Sites Society, Long Hill, Rowley, Massachusetts.

Bibliography

Barron, David P. and Mason, Sharon. *The Greater Gungywamp,* Noank, CT, 1991.

Boland, Charles Michael. *They All Discovered America,* Doubleday, NY, NY, 1961.

Bradford, Ernle. *The Sword and the Scimitar,* G.P. Putnam's Sons, 1974.

Bradley, Michael. *Holy Grail Across the Atlantic,* Hounslow Press, Willowdale, Ontario, Canada, 1988.

Bronasted, Johannsen. *The Vikings,* Penguin Books, Baltimore, MD, 1960

Drake, Samuel Adams. A *Book of New England Legends and Folklore,* Little, Brown and Company, Boston, MA, 1984.

Fell, Barry. *Saga America,* Times Books, NY, NY, 1980.

Godfrey, William S. Jr. *The Archaeology of the Old Stone Bill in Newport,* American Antiquity XVII, 1951.

Hakluyt. *Zeno Narrative - 1558, The Voyage of the Zeno Brothers,* Vol. 50, 1873.

Goodwin, William B. *The Ruins of Great Ireland in New England,* Meador, Boston, MA, 1946.

Holland, Hjalmar R. *Explorations in America Before Columbus,* Twayne, NY, NY, 1956.

Jones, Evan and Robbins, Roland W. *Hidden America,* Knopf, NY, NY, 1959.

Longman, Byron. *The World's Last Mysteries - Who Really Discovered the New World,* Reader's Digest Association, Inc., Pleasantville, NY, 1977.

Mavor, James W. and Dix, Byron E. *Manitou, Stone Structures Reveal New England Native Civilization,* Lindisfarne Press, Great Barrington, MA, 1991.

Means, Philip Answorth. *The Newport Tower,* NY, NY, 1942.

Morison, Samuel Eliot. *The European Discovery of America - The Northern Voyages,* Oxford University Press, NY, NY, 1971.

Norroena, Society. *The Flatey Book,* NY, NY, 1906.

Palfrey, John C. *History of New England,* 1858.

Pohl, Frederick. *The Lost Discovery,* Norton, New York, NY, 1952.

Robinson, John J. *Dungeon, Fire, and Sword, The Knights Templar in the Crusades,* M. Evans & Co., Inc., New York, NY, 1991.

Sinclair, Andrew. *The Sword and the Grail,* Crown Publishers, New York, NY, 1992.

Supreme AWQAF Council. *A Brief Guide to the Dome of the Rock,* Jerusalem, 1956.

Trento, Salvatore Michael. *The Search for Lost America - The Mysteries of the Stone Ruins,* Contemporary Books, Inc., Chicago, IL, 1978.

Whittall, James P. Jr. *Myth Makers, Epigraphic Illusion in America,* E.S.-R.S. Epigraphic Series, No. 1, 1990.

Whittall, James P. Jr. *Early Sites Research Society Bulletins,* Volume 6, No. 1; Volume 7, No. 2; Volume 10, No. 2; Volume 11, No. 1; Volume 12, No. 1; Volume 13, No. 1.

Wright, Thomas. *Saint Brendan, A Legend of the Sea,* Percy Society, London, England, 1884.